Authentic Diversity

Authentic Diversity

How to Change the Workplace for Good

Michelle Silverthorn

Routledge
Taylor & Francis Group

A PRODUCTIVITY PRESS BOOK

First published 2020
by Routledge
600 Broken Sound Parkway #300, Boca Raton FL, 33487

and by Routledge
2 Park Square, Milton Park, Abingdon, Oxon, OX14 4RN

Routledge is an imprint of the Taylor & Francis Group, an informa business

ISBN: 9780367374518 (hbk)
ISBN: 9780367085674 (pbk)
ISBN: 9780429023071 (ebk)

Typeset in Garamond
by Deanta Global Publishing Services Chennai, India

For my parents and my sister – thank
you for giving me the world.

Contents

About the Author

Michelle Silverthorn is a recognized organizational diversity expert and in-demand keynote speaker. The Founder & CEO of Inclusion Nation, Michelle works with clients across industries to design inclusive spaces centered on equity, belonging, and authenticity. A graduate of Princeton University and the University of Michigan Law School, Michelle lives in Chicago with her husband and their two daughters. Learn more about Michelle and her work at michellesilverthorn.com.

Acknowledgments

Writing a book takes a village, and I am lucky that I have a tremendous one. Thank you to my Taylor & Francis editor, Kristine Mednansky, who believed in this book from the beginning and ushered it to its conclusion. To my research assistants, Lubna El-Gendi, Jeremy Nichols, and Abigail Feenstra, thank you for answering my late-night emails and my emergency requests, and my messages that sometimes were only sent in emojis and question marks. To my family, thank you for your unceasing love. And, finally, to Jasmine and to all the Jasmines out there. I wrote this for you. I do this for you. I will never stop changing the world for you.

Chapter 1

Hello from the 70th Floor

It's 9 a.m. on a Monday morning. I walk into the 70th-floor lobby of a steel and glass skyscraper in, well, it could be any city in the world. But let's say this one is Chicago. It's where I live. Beautiful view of the lake, standard. Glass doors, oak desks, pictures, prizes, and awards. And look, it's you, workplace leader, walking out to greet me. We'll be spending the morning together because you, workplace leader, just got some very bad news.

Maybe you released your diversity numbers on Friday at 4 pm because you knew what the reaction would be and you did your best to hide the numbers as much as you could.

Maybe your organization is being sued by a woman who was harassed out of the workplace.

Maybe you had a superstar group of employees of color who told you last week that they're all leaving together.

Maybe a client called and said they wanted more diversity on the team you're sending them and you realized you had no one to send. Or you did have one person to send (and just one), except you're already sending them to the other client who made an identical request earlier. Or you did find

1

someone to go and they explained how offensive it was to only ever be used as the token, and you didn't understand what that meant.

Maybe a minority executive you were heavily recruiting turned you down, and when you asked her why, she was frank: "Why would I come somewhere where no one looks like me?"

Maybe you read the news that morning and saw that one of your stores had a problematic product, or an offensive commercial, or kicked out someone who just wanted to sit down and read a newspaper. Except that person was Black.

Maybe someone made a comment in a meeting. Maybe someone sent an email. Maybe someone sent a dozen emails. Maybe that someone was you.

All of these are possible. Sometimes they happen. But sometimes you are someone else. You are an Indian nurse, a Black manager, a Latino executive, or a woman partner, and you want others to see what you're seeing, to understand what you go through every day – especially the White men who dominate the management and executive positions at your workplace. You want them to see that no matter how much they say inclusion matters, diversity counts, or how many programs, dinners, and scholarships they have, leadership looks the same as it did 100 years ago.

See, most of the time, the reason I get a call from you is that you have had enough. You may be the CEO. You may be the head of talent development, people, recruiting, or even diversity, inclusion, and belonging. You may be a mid-level manager. You may be a straight, cisgender, White male executive without a disability. No matter who you are, and whatever level you are at in your organization, you *are* a leader, a leader who sees the problem with workplace diversity and wants to know how to solve it.

That's when you meet me. I walk up to you, you shake my hand, and we head into your office to try to change the world because that is exactly what we are going to do together.

I am Michelle Silverthorn. I specialize in equity, inclusion, and organizational change. In the next few chapters, I am going to outline precisely why we are stuck on workplace equity and what actions you as a leader can take to change that. I don't care what your title is. I don't care if you started 30 years ago or this morning. You are a leader in how you act with, talk about, and deliver results to the people you work with. You have the power to make diversity matter for good.

This book applies to *all* leaders. However, many of the lessons we will discuss – including ones about race, anti-Blackness, and privilege – especially apply to the leaders who have long been running the American workplace – White men. The changes I want to see leaders make start at the very top, with people who have the clout to bring others on board and the resources to make change happen. Throughout corporate America, those people are almost always White men. If you're one of those White men reading this book, then recognize that much of what I say is intended for you.

Giving You the Right Tools to Solve the Problem

I don't have any cute acronyms. I'm not here to sell you anything. I'm not going to make you sit through 180 pages of fluff to read 5 pages of a half-baked solution – because I'm tired, too. I'm tired of attending the same meetings, getting frustrated at the same stalled progress, sitting on the same ineffective panels, and hearing the same complaints over and over again. It's not enough to see a problem or acknowledge that a challenge exists. I don't want leaders who stand back and complain; I want leaders who stand up and make a change.

In these pages, I'm going to deliver to you the tools to successfully transform your stalled diversity outcomes. These are the same tools I share with leadership teams and organizations across the globe. I study their companies and their culture. I tell them the challenges I see based both on my experiences with similar organizations and on my research, writing, and professional work. Then we work on designing solutions together centered on equity.

My work delivers results. Whether cultural shifts, honest conversations, strategy design, hiring plans, or talent development models, the work I do with my clients produces the change they are looking for and change they didn't know they needed. What I share with them is what I'm going to share with you today – the new rules for equity.

It's Time for New Rules

We have long been trying to make progress using the old rules of *diversity*, but it's a new decade in a new century in a world permanently changed by a pandemic, and today we need new rules of *equity* to truly transform the workplace into one of *inclusion*. These new rules center on one simple truth: people matter. That woman who just quit her job isn't a statistic, a number, a minority, or a beneficiary of affirmative action. She isn't "the diverse one." She is a person – a person who wanted to succeed – and you, as a leader, failed her. You'll keep failing her, and everyone who comes after her, if you're not willing to change the old rules of diversity you're leading with.

Try to read this book all at once. On your lunch break, after dinner, on a flight, in your office between student visits, on the elliptical, on the studio back lot, after you've put your kids to bed – whenever and wherever you can. People are struggling, suffering, and leaving. The more time we waste, the more people become statistics, and the more hopeless change seems to be.

Let's get started. And I do mean "start": I will give you your shoes, your walking stick, and your map, but the hike is all yours to take. You know the terrain. You know the people walking with you. The question is, "Where are you going?" That's what this book is for.

Diversity is Where We Start

You're about to read a book on diversity, equity, and inclusion. What do I mean when I say those terms? In the broadest sense, *diversity* refers to the many ways our individual identities differ. These differences affect our perspectives about the world, how we are perceived by others, how we are included or excluded in our environments, and whether we are given or denied certain benefits of membership in the society in which we are in.

One way to think about diversity, but by no means the only way, is through three main dimensions of diversity: primary, secondary, and tertiary. Let's focus on the primary dimensions of diversity. Primary dimensions of diversity are the ones we typically have no control over, like age, ability status, race, ethnicity, gender and gender identity, and sexual orientation. Here, for example, is how I, Michelle Silverthorn, might break down the primary dimensions of my identity.

Age: At the time of this writing, I am 37 years old, which in and of itself can lead to bias. Ageism in the form of negative bias against people older or younger than us is a common issue in the workplace.

Ability status: I am currently not a person with a disability, which means I do not have any cognitive, developmental, intellectual, or physical disabilities that make it more difficult for me to do certain activities or interact with the world.

Race: I am Black. Race is a construct based on observable physical characteristics, like my skin color, that have acquired socially significant meaning. Because I am married to a White man, my children can be considered biracial, multiracial, or mixed – although in the United States they might simply be called Black.

Ethnicity: Ethnicity is made up of cultural factors such as language, religion, and nationality. Although people might call me African American, this term is often reserved for the descendants of enslaved Africans who were forced to come to the United States prior to the 20th century. My background, however, is Jamaican and Trinidadian. I immigrated to America when I was 17 years old, so I identify ethnically as a West Indian American.

It can be easy to confuse race and ethnicity because they are both constantly evolving constructs. Is "Asian" a race or ethnicity? Are people from Bangladesh and Russia both considered "Asian?" Many Latinx people will check either White or Black on the U.S. census, not based on the color of their skin but based instead on how they counter discrimination.[1] Do they counter it by identifying with a racial majority or a racial minority? As a leader, pay attention to how discussions of race and ethnicity evolve over your life, who determines which words are used for which groups, and whose agendas are being promoted when they do.

Gender and gender identity: Gender refers to the attitudes, feelings, roles, and behaviors a particular culture associates with biological sex. Gender identity is one's innermost concept of oneself as male, female, a blend of both, or neither. I identify as a cisgender female, which means my gender identity aligns with the sex I was assigned at birth. Only one person gets to determine my gender identity, and that's me.

As a cisgender woman, I use the female pronouns she, her, and hers. If I were non-binary, I might use gender-neutral pronouns like "they" and "them." The best way to learn what pronouns someone prefers is to ask them. Even better, create a norm in your workplace that people identify by the gender pronouns in their email signatures, website bios, or meeting introductions.

Many people choose not to identify as either male or female. They are non-binary and may identify as bigender (having two or more genders), agender (having no gender), third-gender (having a gender that is neither male nor female), or gender fluid (moving between genders). Those whose gender identities match the sex opposite to the one they were assigned at birth are transgender. Please note that people can be transgender without taking hormones or having surgery. Transgender identity goes far beyond medical change.

Sexual orientation: I am a straight or heterosexual female, which means I am attracted to men. That is my sexual orientation. Other people are gay (men attracted to men), lesbian (women attracted to women), bisexual (attracted to both men and women), pansexual (attracted to all gender identities), asexual (lacking sexual interest), and so on. The full spectrum of gender identities and sexual orientations outside of straight and cisgender is known as the LGBTQ+ community.

Intersectionality: Taken together, all of the above elements constitute intersectional me: Michelle, who is Black, female, straight, an immigrant, and a mother, all the overlapping and interconnecting identities that construct me. Kimberlé Crenshaw, who was the first to name and formalize intersectional theory, has defined the term "intersectionality" to mean the ways various components of our individual identities intersect and are viewed, understood, and treated in relation to one another.[2] Intersectionality is how we get specific about identity.

Inclusion is Where We're Going

My focus in this book is on making the workplace both fair and welcoming to those who have historically faced discrimination for any one aspect of their identity – which is where inclusion comes in. Inclusion means creating environments where any individual or group can feel welcomed, respected, supported, valued, and able to fully participate. Inclusion means that people who are different can come together with their unique experiences, preferences, and strengths, without assimilating those salient identities that they have. Here's another way to put it. I love this quote from diversity expert, Vernā Myers: "Diversity is being invited to the party. Inclusion is being asked to dance."[3] No matter what you look like, sound like, or identify as. Your differences matter, and you are

welcome here. You are valued here. You are allowed to succeed here. You belong here. That's inclusion.

But how do we get there? How do we ensure fair treat-
ment, access, opportunity, and advancement for all people,
while eliminating the barriers that have prevented the full par-
ticipation of many of them? To have inclusion, you must also
have equity.

Equity Is How We Get There

Have you seen the two side-by-side pictures of the three Black
boys of different heights standing on crates to watch a baseball game over a fence?[4] The first picture is called "equality."
Equality means giving all three boys the same size crates to
stand on, even though the boys are of different heights. Only
the two taller boys get to see the game that way. The second
picture is called "equity." Equity means giving each boy a crate
that matches his height. The shortest boy gets the tallest crate,
the one in the middle gets the medium-sized crate, and the
tallest boy gets the smallest crate. All the boys get to watch the
game – behind a fence.

The pictures provide an easy answer to what equity is.
Equity means giving people the resources they need in order
to succeed. But is that enough? Because that means we still
have the fence up to block the baseball game. The only solution for the boys to see the baseball game is to help them
peek over the fence. It isn't to change the height of the fence.
It isn't to remove the fence. Heck, it isn't even to *let the boys
inside the stadium.* Instead, the picture suggests that equity
only means providing people with the tools of success. This
is a comforting view to those in power because it means we
don't need to change anything about the world – we just need
to give the people accessing it a boost.

That's why giving the boys those crates is only half the
work of equity. The other half of equity is understanding why

the barriers exist in the first place. The other half is changing the system itself. That's *real equity*. Dismantling systems of inequality and oppression that prevent marginalized individuals from success.

I don't want three Black boys who have to stand outside to watch a baseball game. I want three Black boys who walk through those stadium gates, sit down, and take up their space inside. When I say "change the workplace," that is exactly what I mean. If we want a diverse workplace centered on inclusion, then we need to start with equity. We need to eliminate the barriers that inhibit inclusion, and replace them with ones that allow inclusion to take root. Inclusion is our destination. Equity is how we get there. That's how we change the workplace for good.

Which is also why there's one more task I have for you before we start on our journey together. I want to give you a few reality checks on why changing the workplace is much easier to say than to do.

Reality Check #1: This Isn't a Comfortable Book

If you are a White workplace leader, then this book is likely to make you feel very uncomfortable. I'm not going to pat you on the back and say what a great job you've done. We have become far too comfortable failing at equity. Too many leaders are OK with saying, "Well, that's just the way it is!" Or we make the following excuses:

> "There aren't enough qualified people!"
> "We don't have the time to train them!"
> "They aren't applying for the job!"
> "We have to hire and hire fast!"
> "They wouldn't have cut it here anyway!"

Let me repeat: those are excuses. They are rationalizations to avoid putting in the hard, self-reflective, and often painful work of diversity, equity, and inclusion. Leveling the playing field means incurring the wrath of those who have been winning on that uneven playing field all this time. Are you ready for that anger? That resentment? I want you to be honest.

Are you ready to get uncomfortable? Are you ready to be challenged? Are you ready to do more than pay lip service to diversity? Are you ready to be held accountable? Are you ready to put your money where your convictions are? Are you ready to be bold? Be brave? Are you ready to think about the world differently? If you're not ready then get ready because I want you to change the workplace, and changing the workplace takes hard work. It takes courageous leaders standing up to say this may be the way we've always done it, but here is the way we are going to change it.

Reality Check #2: "They're So Well-Intentioned"

Do you know how many times I have heard people say that their leadership, their managers, or their employees are all "well-intentioned"? I know we do it because we think words like "racism," "discrimination," "sexism," and "transphobia" apply only to bad people. They do not apply to good, "well-intentioned" folks. "If you just knew their hearts, you'd know" is the excuse I'll hear. Well, I can't know their hearts. Their actions are all I have to go by. Show me the proof of good intentions – because that person who just sent the email excoriating your organization for its lack of gender diversity doesn't care if your leaders were well-intentioned; she cares about what they *did*.

Simply put, assuming everyone is well-intentioned prioritizes one person's comfort over another person's pain. The focus has to be on the impact of the actions: the homogeneity that results from well-intentioned choices that you and your recruiters have made; the inequity that results from well-intentioned policies that you and your managers have put into place; the exclusion that results from well-intentioned actions that you and your employees have performed.

Look at the data. Look at the numbers. Look at the exit interviews. Look at who is staying and who is leaving. And realize this: falling back on "well intentioned" will leave you right where you started, focused on the successful majority and how well intentioned they are, rather than on the marginalized minority and how excluded they have become.

Reality Check #3: I am Black, Black, Black

This book is written by a Black woman in the American workplace. I will tell a lot of stories about being Black. I will talk about anti-Black racism in America. I will talk about my own journey to antiracism. I will tell my story. That story is from the perspective of a marginalized identity in today's society, a Black woman in America.

But there are many other marginalized identities. I use terms such as "marginalized" (those who have been historically excluded due to their identity from power structures in their society), "minority" (those who are disadvantaged in relation to the dominant social group, the "majority"), and "person of color" (a person who is not considered White), "BIPOC" (Black, Indigenous, and People of Color, to acknowledge the unique experiences of discrimination faced by Indigenous people and Black people), knowing that they are messy, imperfect terms that encapsulate millions of people in America at the intersection of particular cultures, races, ethnicities, genders, orientations, beliefs, families, histories, and stories.

I want to confess this at the beginning because much of the challenge I see with diversity is that we are so non-specific in our efforts, often deliberately because it is harder to be specific, so we speak as if every marginalized professional has the same challenges. It's also why we use the term "diverse" so we can be broader rather than specific. It is comfortable to be broader; it's much more uncomfortable to be specific. That's why terms continue to evolve, using anti-Blackness rather than racism for example, to ensure that we are specific in what actions we are discussing and what solutions we are putting into place.

I will try to be specific. I am a Black, straight, cisgender 37-year-old immigrant woman without a disability speaking from a Black, straight, cisgender 37-year-old immigrant woman without a disability's perspective. I constantly work to be inclusive in my examples and in my language, so I want to be honest about my lived experiences from the start. I am writing a book about diversity, but I will speak a great deal about race, specifically about Blackness. I will not wave my hands in the air to distract you while I pretend that my particular lens does not exist. I might not always succeed. That's why you're here to hold me accountable.

But I called this book *Authentic Diversity* for two reasons. First, because "diversity" is still the language of the workplace – for now – and my focus is the workplace. Second, because I get calls from leadership, and, to a person, those calls have similar complaints and concerns. Then I talk to their marginalized employees. And, to a person, those calls have similar complaints and concerns – across organizations, across industries, across cultures, across countries, across identities. Their stories about being excluded, overlooked, and ignored; about the assumptions made about their competence or lack thereof; about accommodations that cannot be made for them but can magically appear for others; about the in-groups that they are not a part of; about the jokes that they have seen sent in emails; about the extra unpaid work they have to do; about the hurtful statements made about them; about the belief that they should be "This" because they look like "That"; about the rules that are never explained to them, but they are expected to compete with; about the competition that is already stacked against them before they even come in the door; about the constant, unending, emotional toll of being a marginalized employee in the workplace.

So no, I cannot and will not speak for everyone. But I can start with one person. I want to start with Jasmine because she's the reason I started this journey. It's her world that I've been working to transform, which is why it's time to meet her. It's time to learn the old rules of diversity, the rules that can no longer stand.

Are you ready to change the workplace? Good. So am I. Let's begin.

Notes

1. https://theconversation.com/the-us-census-bureau-keeps-confusing-race-and-ethnicity-89649
2. www.vox.com/the-highlight/2019/5/20/18542843/intersectionality-conservatism-law-race-gender-discrimination
3. *Myers, V., American Bar Association., & American Bar Association. (2011). Moving diversity forward: How to go from well-meaning to well-doing. Chicago, Ill: ABA Center for Racial & Ethnic Diversity.*
4. https://medium.com/@TriangleCF/everyone-is-talking-about-equity-b513f073c145

Chapter 2

Why We Are Stuck on Workplace Diversity

"Are You OK?"

My long journey with Jasmine starts on Monday, September 29, 2008. Do you remember where you were on that day? I do because September 29, 2008, was my very first day of work. I was fresh out of law school and starting at a prestigious firm in Manhattan. It was also the day that the stock market crashed, losing 777.68 points in one day.[1] Along with dozens of my newly hired colleagues, I soon realized that, with the markets frozen, deals weren't getting done, loans weren't getting issued, and clients certainly weren't interested in having some green, first-year attorneys work on the few projects that they did have.

What does a firm do when it over hires employees? It lays them off. In one day. Hundreds of my colleagues were told that morning that they had to be out of their offices by midday. Some cried, some screamed, some laughed, some were silent, some drank tequila, some were escorted out by security, and at the end of the day, they were all gone. They cried, they screamed, they laughed, they were silent, they drank tequila, they were escorted out by security, and, at the end of the day, they were gone. If you've never lived through a layoff, consider yourself lucky. I wouldn't wish that experience on my worst enemy.

But here's what I remember most about that day. Not the tears, not the anger, not the single phone call to my officemate to have her come into the partner's office to hear the news. No, it was that afternoon, after everyone had left, and the rest of us were wandering around shell-shocked like we had just left a blast zone. I remember walking back from the bathroom and seeing a White male partner in the office three doors down from mine turn his head to me and ask a simple question, "Are you OK?"

I don't remember what I said. I probably nodded, smiled, and went back to my office to cry. But I remember that it was the first time he had asked me anything in the four months that I had worked on his floor. For four months, I had walked past his office, and he had never once said, "Hello." For four months, I had seen him in the elevator, by the bathrooms, or talking with our shared assistant, and I hadn't shared a single word with him or the other three White male partners who shared his floor. Did my presence make them uncomfortable? Did they think it wasn't worth talking to me because I'd be leaving soon? (Even before the layoffs, our industry had a notorious churn rate, hence the large numbers of hires.) Was there something so abhorrent about me that they couldn't bring themselves to share a simple greeting?

After his brief expression of concern, we remained friendly at the office. We chatted in the elevator, confessed that we were intimidated by our assistant, and we even had coffee together once. For the year and a half that I remained at this firm, I felt like there was someone who wanted me to be there. All it took was a simple question, "Are you OK?"

After I left New York, I moved to Chicago with my new husband to fulfill the always-true rule about people from the American Midwest – they go back. My husband is from Michigan, and Chicago was his dream, so to Chicago we went. I moved to a different law firm, and I worked there for two years before I realized that I wanted a new home. I didn't want to practice; I wanted to teach. I did find a new home. It was a small organization with a very long name, the Illinois Supreme Court Commission on Professionalism. We had an enormous mandate – teaching 90,000 attorneys in Illinois to be civil with each other. For the next six years, that is exactly what I did.

But I didn't just travel around the state speaking to lawyers. I would also speak at law schools and to groups of law students about diversity and inclusion. That's how I met Jasmine.

The Rules of Diversity and Inclusion

When you teach diversity, you learn to follow the rules. We all know about rules, right? We've been told to follow the rules since we were kids. Don't run in the hall. Don't speak too loudly. Color between the lines. Keep your voice down. Don't take up too much space. All the rules that govern our lives.

You know what else has rules? Diversity and inclusion. At least talking about it does – rules like *Make the business case for diversity and inclusion. Money talks. Don't make anyone too uncomfortable. Don't be too radical with your ideas for change. Don't be too honest. Don't tell anyone they're wrong.*

I know about those rules because when I used to teach diversity and inclusion, I would follow those rules. I would talk to my groups, and I would make sure I stayed in my little sandbox. You don't want to ruffle too many feathers. I wouldn't say any of what I was doing was soft-pedaling diversity, but I would say that it was coloring very carefully between the lines.

But you know when I would really follow the rules? When I talked with Black people. As any Black person reading this book knows, we know how the game is played; what we are expected to do to succeed. We have to follow the rules. When we don't follow the rules is when we fail. We know how to build our own crates so we can see over the fence to watch a baseball game.

So, when Black people asked me how to succeed, I would tell them the things that we are supposed to say. Change your hair; change your accent; don't talk about your background, your schools, your cultures, your clothes. Change your tone of voice, your way of walking even, the pictures you put on your desk, the music you listen to in the background. Remember to work harder, but don't complain. Remember to walk carefully, but don't stumble. Respectability politics! Because the second you stumble, someone will look at you and think, "She's not right for here." Those are the rules.

"How Long?"

Then one day, I sat on a diversity crisis panel. If you don't know what a crisis panel is, it's when a crisis related to diversity happens in an organization, and it's like, "Avengers! Assemble."

This one was at a law school. And assemble we did. A professor had used a racial slur in class, and so the school called on their best to run a crisis town hall. Except, the town hall was attended solely by those who needed it least – the handful of Black students in the school, almost all of whom were women.

So it goes in the diversity world, which meant, inevitably, the conversation turned to what Black people, and in particular Black women, needed to do in order to succeed in corporate America. And like the many people before us, we gave them the rules. We were honest. We were frank. "If you want to succeed, here's what you need to do." All the ways you need to change who you are, to adopt a new persona, in order to succeed. Your hair, clothes, jewelry, family, emotions, tone of voice, accent, way of working, way of socializing, way of speaking. None of that is good enough. Blow out your hair; wear a suit; make sure you keep your laughs low; make sure you keep your smiles on; wear the pearl necklaces and the small earrings, minimal makeup, not too loud, not too abrasive, not too ethnic, and above all, not too you. You know what I mean. You'll make it. As long as you change.

What a coward I was.

We talked like that for about 45 minutes. I saw a lot of head nods, and at one point, I thought, "These young people get it. They're going to be fine." And while I was busy patting myself on the back, I saw a trembling raised hand in the back of the room. It was a young Black woman. We smiled at her. She stood up. We asked her name. She said it was Jasmine. But she was barely able to get it out because Jasmine was crying – tears streaming down her face. She looked at the three of us sitting there and asked two simple words.

"How long?"

I looked at my two fellow Avengers. I turned back to Jasmine and asked, a bit confused, "How long what?" Jasmine took a steadying breath. She wiped her face. Then she asked again in a stronger voice.

"How long? How long do I have to do this? To mask? To cover? To code-switch? To change? To be someone I'm not?"

She paused.

"I'm Black. I don't want to hide that. When will they just want me for me?"

We three superheroes looked at each other. We looked at Jasmine. Then one of us, and I don't remember who, said very simply: "I am so sorry. For the rest of your career."

Because those are the rules.

But here's the kicker. Even if Jasmine did all of that, it probably wouldn't matter because her ceiling isn't made of glass – it's made of solid concrete. To paraphrase Ms. Nina Simone, Jasmine was destined to be "young, Black, and passed over."

The Ballad of Jasmine and Dave

It's graduation day! Congratulations to Jasmine and Dave. They are both graduating today, and everyone is thrilled. At Jasmine's school, parents, relatives, and teachers stream around the hallowed campus grounds, pride-filled faces, looking at the hope of the next generation as they venture into the world. And Jasmine is especially happy because in one month, she'll be starting work at a wonderful mid-sized American company called Devlin.

At Dave's school, parents, relatives, and teachers stream around the hallowed campus grounds, pride-filled faces, looking at the hope of the next generation as they venture into the world. And Dave is especially happy because in one month, he'll be starting work at a wonderful mid-sized American company called Devlin.

This is the Ballad of Jasmine and Dave.

A few weeks pass, and Jasmine and Dave start at Devlin. They're in the same department. Finance, accounting, investing, law, tech, pick an industry, any industry. The story is the same. Jasmine and Dave are on the same floor. Let's even start them on the very same day because that is the day that their paths diverge.

It starts with the socializing. Early on, Dave creates social bonds with White male executives, sales managers, marketing directors, and partners. They invite him out places, they meet up for drinks in their shared neighborhoods, they stop by his office to catch up, they pop their head in his door when they're leaving, they send around jokes and emails, they talk with him via video chat, and even though everyone is extraordinarily busy, they make him feel like he's part of the team. They ensure that he feels he belongs and can succeed there. They don't need to ask him, "Are you OK?" because that's not what they do. It's not part of their culture. He's working well, and he's a good guy. He's the right fit. That's all they need to know.

That's how Dave gets the "good work" – the quality, skill-building projects that lead to higher quality, more visible projects with senior leaders and prominent clients. The work that looks great on his evaluations. The work that gets remembered by management. The work that puts him on the track to success. It's not just because Dave is good at what he does. He is. It's also because when he socializes with the White male leaders, they talk about work – the work Dave is getting, the work he's not getting, the people he should be working with, the clients he should be recruiting, the pipelines he should be developing, the accounts worth his time, the projects he should be investing in, the likes and dislikes of some of the managers, the behind-the-scenes gossip, and the secrets of success.

This is all great for Dave, not just because of what he gets out of it professionally, but because these are *his kind of guys* – the kind he would have been friends with back in college. It's not easy – he has to put in the long hours, miss his kids' activities, and deal with micro-managers – but throughout Dave feels like he belongs here. He feels that way when he walks down the hall and sees the framed pictures of all the White men who have been CEOs at Devlin. When he attends Devlin's all-employee meetings where the White male leaders share the company's outlook for the year. When he looks through the company's history and sees that all the great names listed are those of White men. When he gets his projects and sees that almost all the team leads, and those whom they report to, are White men. And if any of those White men did ask him, "Are you OK?" the question wouldn't take Dave by surprise at all.

Then there's Jasmine. Jasmine doesn't get invited to these casual social meet-ups. The men don't drop by her office to see if she's busy or if she wants a chat. She doesn't live in the same neighborhood as they do or share any external social networks with them. They may nod when they pass her in the hallway, but that's it. She sees them going into Dave's office, and she tries to lean in. She reaches out. She introduces herself. She asks what she can help with. But it is always on her to do the work. She asks them out for coffee, she offers to meet up for lunch, or she smiles and says, "Hello" in the elevator. She is always the one asking, and the truth is, even when she does, there's no real follow-up and no real engagement.

But Jasmine remembers. She remembers that panel. She remembers talking about the rules, so she decides to follow them. She comes in to work with her hair in a weave or blowout, wearing the right suit, the right watch, and the right shoes. She reads the business and leadership books so she'll have something to talk about with them. They never worry about doing any extra work so they'll have something to talk about with her. It is always her stepping into their culture, never them stepping into hers. So she doesn't talk about her neighborhood, her church, the nephew she's raising, or the old episode of *Martin* she just saw. She mimics how the White men compete in boardrooms. She imitates how they talk with their clients. She studies how they try to out-do each other. She tries to exude their confidence, their swagger, and their absolute certainty that their place is right here.

Jasmine follows all the rules. But throughout, she feels like she doesn't belong here. She feels that way when she walks down the hall and sees the framed pictures of all the White men who have been CEOs at Devlin. When she attends Devlin's all-employee meetings where the White male leaders share the organization's outlook for the year. When she looks through the organization's history and sees that all the great names listed are those of White men. When she gets her projects and sees that almost all the team leads, and those whom they report to, are White men. And if any of those White men did ask her, "Are you OK?" the question would shock her.

Now it's evaluation time. Dave and Jasmine receive their reviews. They both receive good evaluations because this organization, like many in corporate America, still has supervisors who are deeply uncomfortable delivering feedback. But even in that deep discomfort, the feedback is different. Dave gets a lot more specific, targeted, growth-oriented feedback, while Jasmine's is a lot more "Atta girl! Love what you're doing. Keep up the good work."

So Jasmine continues, but she doesn't really feel like a part of the workplace. She doesn't feel supported. She has a lot of new ideas, but when she brings them up to leadership, they don't go anywhere. She keeps working long hours; she goes to lunches and dinners; and she makes sure to attend sales trainings, networking events, coaching lessons, and employee resource group meetings. Plus, she keeps doing the work. She comes early, she stays late, because she believes what they say at Devlin – working hard is the way to succeed.

Now it's about five years in. It's time for a big promotion, the one that will eventually lead to the director-level position that both Dave and Jasmine want. Jasmine looks around her and thinks, "I've been working just as hard as everyone here, my evaluations have been great, clients and customers think I'm doing good work, I am getting them results, I am succeeding here. I am ready for this." She walks into that staff meeting or that evaluation session, or she sits and waits at her phone for someone to call. They have to call. She's done exactly what she was supposed to do to succeed. She followed all of the rules.

The call comes. The announcement is made. But it's not for Jasmine. It's for Dave. Dave is the one promoted. Dave is the one now on the superstar track. Dave is heading to the C-suite. Not now, not five years from now, but eventually. All signs point to yes.

Jasmine sits in her office, shell-shocked. She picks up the phone. She types an email. Or she walks into a manager's office. Like that day five years ago when she met me, she asks a very simple question again: "Why?" And in this fictional organization in which she has spent the formative years of her career, her boss tells her the truth.

"Jasmine, no one knows you. No one talks about you in meetings. These evaluations are fine but not great. You haven't been working on really good projects, and honestly, there have been some concerns about your performance. And your tone."

What concerns? She works long hours. She goes to all the work events. She's a mentor. She's even on the company webpage touting women and diversity.

"But that's not enough," her boss laughs. "How did you not know that wasn't enough? Jasmine, look at Dave. Dave got the great work. Dave went to the meetings that mattered. Dave had the right clients. Dave knew people around here. People talk about Dave. Dave is clearly committed to success. And you, Jasmine – we gave you the chance, but you just don't want it. You're not doing enough to succeed here."

So Dave gets promoted to leader, while Jasmine has to decide whether she's going to stay where she is and keep treading water or whether she is going to leave.

Twenty-five years later, Dave does make it to the C-suite at Devlin. At age 52, Dave is now a well-compensated, highly admired, and oft-rewarded executive at one of the largest companies in the state. Meanwhile Jasmine has been gone for 15 years. She realized the same truth that thousands of Black men and women learn every day – even when you play by the rules, you still lose.

That is the Ballad of Jasmine and Dave. And that is the reality for many marginalized professionals in the workplace. That is where the rules have gotten us. We have collectively spent billions of dollars on diversity initiatives, yet we haven't done the hard work to keep the Jasmines of the world in the workplace, and when she leaves, we throw up our hands in the air and ask why.

Over and over again, I have met hundreds of Jasmines. They keep on sharing the same story with me because the companies in which they work are all living under the same old rules of diversity – the same rules, the same story, the same ending, every single time. No matter how much Jasmine plays by the rules, she still loses. Just look at the statistics.

Diversity in Corporate America: By the Numbers

It's hard to compile corporate diversity numbers, especially reliable ones. Less than 4% of Fortune 500 companies report their workforce race and gender demographics. Moreover, the vast majority of companies that do report their full diversity numbers are in the tech sector.[2] And many of the thousands of mid-size to large companies in corporate America do not collect demographic data at all. The existing research, however, can help us paint a fairly accurate picture of the workforce – one that many minority employees can tell you firsthand is true. As one observer notes,

> Where workforce data is available, it often illustrates the slow progress in building racial and ethnic diversity into the C-suite. Too frequently the representation of non-White employees and women rapidly diminishes with rank.[3]

This drop-off in diversity from entry level to management level is starkly illustrated by following the trajectory of different groups from entry level to management positions. A 2018 study conducted by McKinsey and LeanIn.Org of 279 companies employing more than 13 million people provides the following data:

> White men make up 35% of entry-level hires, 45% of manager positions, 51% of senior manager/director positions, 57% of VP positions, 64% of SVP positions, and 68% of C-suite positions.

For men of color, those statistics are, respectively, 16%, 17%, 14%, 12%, 10%, and 10%.

For White women, 30%, 27%, 26%, 24%, 21%, and 18%.

For women of color, 18%, 12%, 9%, 7%, 5%, and 4%.

A full 86% of C-suite positions are occupied by White workers.[4]

While some advocates have pushed the idea that "increasing the diversity of directors encourages companies 'to be more open to hiring women and minority employees' ... a highly diverse board does not necessarily mean that the executives who run a company are – or ever become – truly diverse."[5]

To the contrary, a diverse board can too often serve "as a smokescreen to conceal just how White a company's leaders (the CEO and his team) are."[6] As one scholar notes,

> the truth of the matter is that the biggest problem related to corporate diversity and inclusion is not the boardroom but the C-suite itself. Many of the same companies that we have hailed for having made such sweeping achievements in the boardroom are batting near zero when it comes to African Americans listed in SEC-required 10-K filings of the top five named/compensated officers in the organization.[7]

In a 2019 article for the Washington Post, journalist Susan Reed chronicled her investigation into the demographic composition of company boards and their C-suites.[8] She noted that Wells Fargo was lauded in 2015 for having an incredibly diverse board of directors: 69% of the directors were female or minority.[9] Yet its executive officers comprised seven men and three women, all White, in 2015. Over 20 years, Wells Fargo barely increased its diversity. In 1995, it had ten male and two female executive officers, all White. The bank's C-suite remains all-White today.[10]

Reed found that Morgan Stanley had a board that was almost 43% diverse, "but its executives were all men: six

Whites and one Asian American."[11] Johnson & Johnson told a similar story: while the organization's board of directors was fairly diverse, "the executive-officer team consisted of five White men and one White woman."[12] To Reed, this relationship between diverse boards and a lack of diversity in the C-suite was evident across many companies:

> In fact, four of the top 10 companies with the most diverse boards had all-White executive officers – nearly twice the rate of all the companies studied. Racial segregation of top management teams was more prevalent in companies with the greatest board diversity.[13]

As of this writing, four of the biggest technology giants – Facebook, Google, Microsoft, and Amazon – have zero Black members on their senior leadership team. Neither does Bank of America, Exxon, or JP Morgan. In total, there are 4 Black CEOs of Fortune 500 companies across the nation. And, again, those are just the companies with data we know.[14]

More data. While Latinx or Hispanic Americans make up 17% of the workforce, they only make up 4.3% of company executives. "The gap between labor force and executive representation is wider among Hispanics than any other group."[15] As for the corporate boards, Latinx directors comprise 2.8% of Fortune 500 board seats. As for intersectionality, Latina directors comprise less than 1% of all board seats.[16]

Want even more data? I'm a lawyer; let's do the ten-year challenge. Do you remember the ten-year challenge? We, as a collective social media-obsessed human race, did it in 2019. You posted a flattering picture of yourself from ten years ago, then you posted a really flattering picture of yourself from now, and you said, "Wow! Look how much I've changed!" Let's do this for the legal profession.

In 2009, 87% of U.S. lawyers were White and 67% of U.S. lawyers were men.

10 years later.

In 2019, 85% of U.S. lawyers were White and 64% of U.S. lawyers were men.[17]

Let's do another illustrative version of the 10-year challenge. Say in 2009, I start as a summer associate – a summer intern with an almost-guaranteed first-year associate position at a law firm – will I make partner in 2019?

In 2009, 47% of summer associates were women, 24% of summer associates were minorities, and 13% of summer associates were women of color.[18]

Let's move forward 10 years to 2019 – 24% of law firm partners are women, 9.5% of law firm partners are minorities, and 3% of law firm partners are women of color.

This is diversity in the legal profession, where 75% of partners are men, and 90.5% of partners are White.[19]

It's not just law. It's commercial real estate with executives who are 83% male and 92% White.[20] It's banking with executives who are 76% male and 75% White.[21] It's tech with executives who are 80% male and 83% White.[22] It's insurance with executives who are 85% male and 96% White.[23]

When I talk about changing diversity in the workplace, these are the numbers I worry about. What happens in that path for a minority employee from entry level to C-suite? Why is it that when we are graduating and hiring thousands of minority professionals, we seem to never find any room for diversity at the top? Why is Dave far more likely to make it into that C-suite than Jasmine? Those are the answers, the hard answers, that we need.

Meanwhile, on the 70th Floor

We're back in your office. And let's say you are a White male leader. I tell about Jasmine. About Dave. About the path to the top that is cut off for people like me. In this fictional office, what might happen next?

Silence. I take a sip of water while I eye the awards behind you, your framed diploma, the photos of you and the mayor, the proud membership you have in your club, the trophy from your most recent team-building exercise, the thank you for your charitable work. Maybe your name isn't Dave, but it really could be. And then I wait for one of three reactions I could get.

Reaction 1. Your mouth purses. You nod. Because Jasmine did leave. So did Michael. And Alejandro. And Keisha. And Johan. And dozens more in your organization who have left. You have never heard this before, this feeling of being isolated and excluded, the microaggressions (we'll talk about those) and stereotype threat (yup, we'll get there too) that Jasmine faced. "No wonder she left!" you shake her head. "We never really wanted her to stay." And I smile. Because you get it. You are all the way on board.

Reaction 2. You purse your lips. You narrow your eyes. Then you turn around to that heavily stocked leadership and management bookshelf behind you. I know what you're going to get before you even reach for it. It's pretty easy to guess as it's the only one of your books to even tangentially address the issue we're talking about. You pull it down and slam it on the table. Then you tap your finger on the picture of Sheryl Sandberg on the back and say, "But she didn't try. She didn't do what she had to do. She didn't lean in." And then you lean back in your chair, cross your legs at your ankles, and you wait. Because somehow you have managed to undermine my entire career with just one sentence.

I smile. Because you've forgotten that I'm still an Avenger. I lean in.

"But she did lean in," I reply.

"No, she didn't," you protest. "She didn't know the right people. She didn't knock on doors. She didn't ask people out for coffee." You point back to the book. "She didn't lean in."

"But she did," I respond. "She did everything you're supposed to do. She leaned all the way in. Trust me, you don't need to tell Black women to lean in. We've been leaning in all our lives."

You look confused. "Then what's the problem?" you ask.

"Are you ready for the rest of the story?" I ask.

You nod and we go on.

That would be almost all of the responses. Well, except for this one.

Reaction 3. "OK," you nod. "But it doesn't have anything to do with rules. She just couldn't connect with the White guys. They weren't friends. Fine. Not everyone gets along. She can go meet up with her people, people she has stuff in common with. Go find a Black woman mentor. Not everyone in this office is a White man."

I nod too. Because I have a secret weapon. I am a super-hero, after all. I have the reason you brought me here in the first place.

"May I?" I ask. You nod.

I reach down and pull my tablet out of my bag. I open a spreadsheet. Your diversity numbers. The numbers of minorities and women at every level of your organization – at the entry-level, at the manager level, at the director level, in the C-suite – that overwhelmingly huge numbers of minorities, especially Black women, that Jasmine could have socialized with instead. I show them to you and I wait.

(Do you need to go get your diversity numbers? I'll wait for you too.)

You look at them. You grimace. Then you nod. "OK, I see." You pause. "So tell me about these old rules."

I smile. "The first one, I think you're pretty familiar with. It's called the business case."

Notes

1. https://money.cnn.com/2008/09/29/markets/markets_newyork/
2. https://fortune.com/2017/06/07/fortune-500-diversity/

3. https://www.proxypreview.org/2019/blog-contributor-articles/ diversity-in-the-c-suite-why-its-time-to-shine-a-light-on-executive-leadership

4. https://www.mckinsey.com/featured-insights/gender-equality/ women-in-the-workplace-2018

5. https://www.washingtonpost.com/outlook/corporate-boards-are-diversifying-the-c-suite-isnt/2019/01/04/c45c3328-0f02-11e9-8938-5898adc28fa2_story.html

6. https://www.washingtonpost.com/outlook/corporate-boards-are-diversifying-the-c-suite-isnt/2019/01/04/c45c3328-0f02-11e9-8938-5898adc28fa2_story.html

7. https://www.blackenterprise.com/ change-the-game-on-c-suite-diversity/

8. In addition to her article, you can read her book, *The Diversity Index: The Alarming Truth about Diversity in Corporate America and What Can be Done about It*, Susan Reed, AMACOM, 2011

9. https://www.washingtonpost.com/outlook/corporate-boards-are-diversifying-the-c-suite-isnt/2019/01/04/c45c3328-0f02-11e9-8938-5898adc28fa2_story.html

10. https://www.nytimes.com/2020/06/06/business/corporate-america-has-failed-black-america.html

11. https://www.washingtonpost.com/outlook/corporate-boards-are-diversifying-the-c-suite-isnt/2019/01/04/c45c3328-0f02-11e9-8938-5898adc28fa2_story.html

12. https://www.washingtonpost.com/outlook/corporate-boards-are-diversifying-the-c-suite-isnt/2019/01/04/c45c3328-0f02-11e9-8938-5898adc28fa2_story.html (the source notes that Johnson and Johnson has racially integrated its "team" since the author's study).

13. https://www.washingtonpost.com/outlook/corporate-boards-are-diversifying-the-c-suite-isnt/2019/01/04/c45c3328-0f02-11e9-8938-5898adc28fa2_story.html

14. https://www.nytimes.com/2020/06/06/business/corporate-america-has-failed-black-america.html

15. https://www.latinousa.org/2020/01/27/hispanicexecs/

16. https://www.latinocorporatedirectors.org/docs/Latino_ Representation_on_F1000_Boards_PDF.pdf

17. https://www.americanbar.org/content/dam/aba/administrative/ market_research/national-lawyer-population-demographics-2009-2019.pdf

18. https://www.nalp.org/uploads/2019_DiversityReport.pdf
19. https://www.nalp.org/uploads/2019_DiversityReport.pdf
20. https://www.naiop.org/-/media/About-NAIOP/Diversity-Resources/August-2013-Commercial-Real-Estate-Diversity-Report.ashx?la=en
21. https://financialservices.house.gov/uploadedfiles/d_i_graphic_final.pdf
22. https://www.eeoc.gov/special-report/diversity-high-tech
23. https://www.americanbar.org/groups/litigation/committees/insurance-coverage/articles/2019/diversity-inclusion-in-insurance-industry/

Chapter 3

Old Rule of Diversity #1. Just Make the Business Case for Diversity

"We have to focus on the money, Michelle."

"Can you talk about how diversity makes good business sense, Michelle?"

"You have studies, right, Michelle? About the business case? Start with those. That'll get everyone on board."

"Michelle, mention that the country's demographics are changing. Talk about Gen Z! That's what they need to know."

I have facilitated many diversity programs over the years and in many of them, the very savvy professionals who book me, who understand how their corporate leaders think, ask me to make the "business case" for diversity. Why should my organization expend time and resources on this? Why does this make financial sense for us?

The "business case" is the beating heart of diversity today. Diversity is a business competency. It should be included in an organization's business strategy. The narrative goes that only companies that truly master diversity can compete at the global stage. Why? Let's talk about that because it helps us understand why we keep falling short when we just make the business case for diversity.

Business Case #1: Everyone Wants Diversity

Diversity matters, this argument grow, because of the demand for it. Clients demand that companies send teams more reflective of their global, multicultural customer base. Customers demand the corporate composition of the companies for which they use their buying power, better reflect customers' own diverse identities. Employees demand that when they interview at organizations, they see diversity of identity throughout the workplace, especially in positions of leadership.

These demands are getting louder and more insistent. I love talking about the youngest generation currently in America, Gen Z, the post 9-11 generation, or, as I like to call them, the "call-out" generation. Because they are not hesitant to post, share, blog, and shame companies who fail to commit to diversity. And leadership is listening. Often, when I get called into an organization, it's because of one of those pressure points being selectively applied to the organization and either a need to implement solutions to have those pressure points ease before they affect the bottom line or a recognition that new markets require new faces to navigate them.

Business Case #2: We Look Really Bad When We Don't Consider Diversity

That's Business Case #1, the demands from clients, customers, and employees. Here's Business Case #2: the fall-out when companies don't put diversity first in their considerations. Let's talk about what I call diversity disasters. There's Dolce & Gabbana in China using, for marketing, a video of a Chinese

woman trying to eat a cannoli with chopsticks. Result? Protests
by models and consumers, cancellation of their fashion show,
and removal of their line from stores throughout China.
And unlike some controversies, this did not blow over. Six
months later, a study by research intelligence firm L2 found
that Chinese consumers were still rejecting Dolce & Gabbana,
including many of the celebrities and influencers who play an
enormous role in increasing public sentiment and purchase
power for the brand.[1]

Of course, Dolce isn't alone, particularly in the fashion
world. There's Gucci and the Blackface sweater[2] (who knew a
Black sweater with cartoonish red lips would be offensive to
Black people?), Prada displaying blackface figurines in its New
York store[3] (who knew blackface would be offensive to Black
people?), a Black child modeling an H&M sweater that read
"Coolest Monkey in the Jungle"[4] (who knew being associated
with monkeys would be offensive to Black people?), the rev-
elation that Moschino called all Black customers in their store,
"Serena"[5] (who knew being called by the same name would
be offensive to Black people?), or Burberry sending an outfit
down the runway featuring a noose (who knew ... you get
the point).[6] Whether it's Kim Kardashian West using the name
"Kimono" for her shapewear[7] or Victoria's Secret's CEO saying
no one wants to see plus-sized models or transgender women
in a "fantasy" show,[8] the fashion world is ripe with one diversity disaster after another.

Fortunately for fashion, they're not alone. Dove featured a
Black woman taking off her shirt to reveal a White woman.[9]
Wycon featured a nail polish called "Thick as a N****a."[10] Tarte
Cosmetics used a meme with a Chinese insult so offensive,
I'm not going to write it here.[11] There's White American model
Karlie Kloss featured in *Vogue* styled like a Japanese woman,[12]
Kendall Jenner solving #BlackLivesMatter with a Pepsi,[13] and
famed indigenous person Johnny Depp hawking Dior perfume
through "an authentic journey deep into the Native American
soul in a sacred, founding, and secular territory."[14]

I look at these ad campaigns and product lines and wonder, "Who is greenlighting this?" There is of course a whisper theory that these brands are doing this on purpose to draw attention to themselves. But unless these multi-billion dollar companies are seeing some sort of spike from sending out racist memes and ads into the world, it's far more likely that when you have a team that is always predominantly White and decisionmakers who are often predominantly male, educated in ways that do not include the experience of marginalized communities, you will get these incidents over and over and over again. And trust me, this is not something a 30-minute cultural sensitivity training can solve. If 14-year-old girls are leaving comments on your Instagram calling you "Racist!" then that is not in any way a "good look" for your brand.

But it's not just the advertising. It's the employees as well. Consider the following scenarios:

A Black doctor wants to help a sick passenger on an airline, and the flight attendants refuse because they don't believe she's a real doctor.[15]

Two Middle Eastern passengers are kicked off a Chicago flight for the crime of speaking Arabic.[16]

An Alaska Airlines employee presses the emergency alarm in the Newark Airport, causing hundreds of people to start fleeing the airport, simply because she thinks two East Asian passengers who were standing, waiting for a flight, were acting suspiciously.[17]

A Black celebrity shops at Sephora, and a White employee calls security.[18]

A Black man calls his mother from the lobby of the Doubletree Hotel in which he is staying, and two White employees call the police.[19]

Two Black men sit at a table in Starbucks, and a White employee calls the police.[20]

A Black family sits to eat dinner, and the restaurant's employees ask the family to move at the request of a White customer.[21]

These are not just memeable incidents that are permanently hashtagged. When your employees are the ones doing it on organization property, you better believe that it's not just social media scorn you'll receive; a lawsuit isn't that far behind. Also, it doesn't even matter if it's on organization property. A White man calls the police on a Black man standing, waiting for a friend, in front of an apartment building. Every article mentions that the White man works for YouTube.[22]

And then of course you have the other perspective. "These aren't that bad." "I know what they *meant* to say." "They aren't from [XYZ country, culture, religion], so how would they know?" "They felt threatened." "The organization fired the person/held diversity training/sent an apology/reached a settlement." "People have moved on and forgotten about it." And of course, my favorite one, "We apologize *if* we offended anyone." You're not apologizing because you believe what you said was wrong. You're only apologizing because of the blowback you received.

To those responses, I have three of my own.

First, not everyone has moved on and your organization's standing among minority groups in this country keeps tanking the more these diversity disasters continue.

Second, you want to hire the most talented diverse professionals? Why would they work for an organization that, when they search online, says the organization discriminated against someone who looks exactly like them?

Third, these actions are never one or two rogue employees, team members, retail workers, or folks in the field. These incidents are almost always endemic of the culture that exists in the organization. It's just the tip of the iceberg. If this is what gets out to the public, what's behind closed doors? What's not being publicized? What's not getting out the door? What does it say about the culture you have in your organization that THIS is the public-facing incident that you get? Whose voices are not being heard? Whose voices aren't even being hired? The buck doesn't stop with them. It stops with you.

Business Case #3: Diversity Makes Us a Lot More Successful

Those are your first two business cases. Diversity matters because of what your customers are demanding. Diversity matters because of what your customers are hashtagging. Then there's Business Case #3. Diversity matters because of what it does for your organization. It makes your organization more successful. I'll share some studies below but I also want you to note as you read them, how broadly "diversity" is used.

In 2009, the American Sociological Association found that companies with the highest levels of racial or gender diversity brought in nearly 15 times more sales revenue than those with the lowest. For every 1% increase in racial or gender diversity, there was an increase in sales revenue of 9% and 3%, respectively.[23]

In 2013, global accounting firm Deloitte found that when employees think their organization is committed to and supportive of diversity and those employees feel included, they innovate more, are more responsive to changing customer needs, and enjoy improved team collaboration.[24] Inclusion also leads to reduced absenteeism plus higher evaluations across the board.

In 2017, McKinsey surveyed 1,000 companies covering 12 countries, measuring not only profitability but also longer-term value creation,[25] and found that companies in the top quartile for racial and ethnic diversity on their executive teams were 35% more likely to have financial returns above companies in the bottom quartile. For gender diversity, that number was 21% and especially true when women executives were in line roles versus staff roles. McKinsey found that these results were driven by diverse companies' ability to attract top talent; improve their customer orientation, employee satisfaction, and decision making; and to secure licenses to operate in certain communities.

The evidence for this business case is overwhelming – and it doesn't end there. Here's what Boston Consulting Group reported in 2013: "Companies that reported above-average diversity on their management teams also reported innovation revenue that was 19 percentage points higher than that of companies with below-average leadership diversity – 45% of total revenue versus just 26%."[26]

Credit Suisse in 2014 noted, "Greater diversity in boards and management are empirically associated with higher returns on equity, higher price/book valuations, and superior stock price performance."[27]

In 2013, *Harvard Business Review* reported, "Employees at [more diverse companies] are 45% likelier to report that their firm's market share grew over the previous year and 70% likelier to report that the firm captured a new market,"[28] and on and on and on and on.

So we know that diversity is good for business. But *why*, exactly? In a 2010 study on the benefits of heterogeneous teams, researchers Katherine Phillips, Katie Liljenquist, and Margaret Neale[29] found that socially different group members go a lot further than just introducing new viewpoints or approaches. Rather, diversity triggers more careful information processing absent in homogenous groups. Interestingly, although the researchers found that the less diverse groups were more confident in their performance and group interactions, they also found that the more diverse groups were most successful at completing their tasks. Phillips and colleagues concluded that this had to do with the extra brainpower it takes for people to navigate diversity. Differences among people can create awkwardness and friction, but that's precisely one reason that it works – because the need to diffuse tension leads to better group problem solving.

It's easy to create a homogenous group of people who think similarly, enjoy similar things, work similar hours, and don't make each other uncomfortable. But it doesn't make them better performers, it doesn't make them better problem solvers, and it means that your organization will perform worse than your peers who embrace that discomfort.

So there you have it. Diversity matters because clients, customers, and employees are demanding it, because of the many missteps we make when we choose not to focus on it, and because it makes our teams smarter, more profitable, and better able to tackle the difficult tasks at hand. That, in a nutshell, is the business case. It is also my number-one Old Rule of Diversity.

Why the Business Case Fails

Why is the business case an old rule? What's wrong with making the business case? Let me tell you what's wrong with it.

Start with the obvious. For a lot of people, the old way of doing things is working just fine. When we all looked like each other. When we all got along with each other. When we didn't have to worry about who wasn't getting access or saying the wrong thing. Where we could make decisions quickly because we knew those decisions were the right ones for our customers. Where we could go out to dinners, drinks, and sports events and all feel right at home. Where we didn't have to pander to people who want extended parental leave or work-from-home policies. Where we worked hard and didn't complain that we weren't getting ahead. Where everyone was treated fairly. Where the workplace didn't feel fraught with tension. Where my name wasn't being splashed across social media as "Not Great Bob." Where we made a hell of a lot of money.

Now these new people are coming in. And we're not getting along. We didn't go to the same schools, and we didn't grow up in the same neighborhoods. They complain that they're not getting ahead, they keep talking about our golf tournament as if there's something wrong with it, they need so much extra work on my part to bring them up to speed, and, frankly, everything was much easier when it was just us.

Also, are you telling me that there's something wrong with me? There's something wrong with the way I've always done things? People like me built this organization. People like me created the space to allow people like them to get in. And now they're "OK, Boomer-ing" me? They're talking about privilege? Do they know where I grew up? So why should they get extra help? Why should they get ahead? It's not fair, it's not right, and it's making me mad.

And what difference has any of this made? News flash. Our leadership is all White, and we are still winning in every market. We didn't promote any women last year, and my take home was still $5 million. The last unicorn start-up had four White men who all shared a dorm room at Stanford, and it was valued at $14 billion. So maybe a few of our clients want diversity, but, hey, they aren't pressing for it, we aren't pushing for it, and, at the end of the day, it isn't affecting our bottom line one bit. Even after all of the diversity scandals that we endured, we remain.

Does any of this sound familiar? If you think about so much of the resentment and the push-back that we have heard on diversity and inclusion, some of it said quietly, some of it sent in accidentally forwarded emails, and some of it shouted so loudly that it's made national news – it's when not everyone is on board for diversity because they don't see the need for it. It's when you tell a leader that diversity makes an organization more profitable. And so they, quite logically, expect that to be the case. "Hire X number of women, and we will see Y increase in profit margins."

But what happens when that Y increase doesn't occur? What happens when angry customers tweet about another racially charged incident even though you know you have spent millions on diversity initiatives? What happens when an Indian-American employee leaves and on the way out she is eager to tell you, someone who has to give her future recommendations in her career, "Of course it had nothing to do with diversity. I just wanted a change." Why would you think anything different than that the old way is working fine, and this focus on the "business case" happens to be a lot of sound and fury signifying absolutely nothing? That's why the business case is an old rule. Because the business case is not enough.

The other problem? This is precisely where "diversity of thought" rears its head. Here's how this goes. Because diversity only matters because of the different perspectives it brings, clearly if I have a room full of different perspectives, even if everyone in that room is a straight, cisgender White male without a disability, then I have a diverse room. If anyone is surprised by how much diversity of thought has taken over the narrative of diversity and inclusion, then they haven't been paying attention.

That's where just making the business case leaves us. An executive once complained to me that all of her organization's diversity programming seemed like a lot of fluff to which I responded, "Of course it does." Because it was. Her organization had produced a diversity video that had only White men talking about why differences matter. Her organization's website had phrases like, "Diversity matters here because we acknowledge a range of experiences." What on earth does that mean? Every living person has a range of experiences.

The business case fails. It fails over and over again. It fails when you as a leader try to paper over identity differences rather than manage conflict. It fails when you try to put a monetary value on identity. It fails when you say the only reason we are doing this is because our customer base is transforming or our clients are demanding it. The business case isn't even a stick. It's a very tiny needle. Every once in a while, it will prick you on your big toe, and you'll say, "Ouch, that hurts." But then you'll shake it off and start walking again. It takes more than a pinprick to bring a giant down, and you know that.

So yes, it will cost money to replace that transgender employee who just quit, and you may not hire that woman when your competitor is offering six months of maternity leave and you're only offering six weeks. But is it really worth upending your entire line of business? Is it really worth the angry emails? Is it really worth taking the time to hire when you needed 10 new engineers yesterday? Is it really worth explaining to your board why you made this decision that looks like poor financial planning in both the short and long-term? Is it really worth the resentment from the majority employees who feel left behind?

The Business Case Is Not Enough

I don't think the business case is dead. Because you are losing people. Because you are making gaffes. Because you are being called out on social media. And because I just showed you all those studies that demonstrate that you do make more money when you commit to diversity – as long as you commit to it.

But I do think the business case is insufficient. Perhaps there are certain parts of your business, particularly for certain global deliverables, where there is a clear correlation between hiring diversity and financial return. But then we're right back to where we started. Is it gender? Is it race? Is it ethnicity? Is it language? Is it education? Is it income? Is it class? Is it veteran status? Is it "thought"? When we say "diversity matters" without getting specific about what diversity matters and why it does, then we run the risk of being stuck exactly where we are, with initiatives that end up being little more than window-dressing; do nothing to move the needle on any meaningful numbers, and make it apparent to the minorities and the majority in your workplace that diversity is lip service again.

Jasmine needs more than the business case. You as a leader need more than the business case. That's an old rule. Let's replace it with a new one.

Notes

1. www.gartner.com/en/marketing/insights/daily-insights/dolce-gabbana-still-canceled-in-china
2. www.wsj.com/articles/gucci-owner-pledges-sensitivity-training-after-Blackface-sweater-11549996946?mod=hp_lead_pos10
3. https://www.cnn.com/style/article/prada-pulls-products-blackface-imagery/index.html
4. https://www.washingtonpost.com/news/arts-and-entertainment/wp/2018/01/19/hm-faced-backlash-over-its-monkey-sweatshirt-ad-it-isnt-the-companys-only-controversy/
5. https://www.vox.com/the-goods/2019/1/16/18185696/moschino-code-word-serena-Black-shoppers-racism
6. https://www.salon.com/2019/02/20/prada-gucci-and-now-burberry-are-brands-under-fire-for-offensive-designs-doing-it-on-purpose/
7. https://www.vox.com/culture/2019/7/1/20677245/kim-kardashian-kimono-backlash-new-name
8. https://www.vogue.com/article/victorias-secret-ed-razek-monica-mitro-interview
9. www.cnbc.com/2017/10/09/dove-faces-pr-disaster-over-ad-that-showed-Black-woman-turning-White.html
10. www.teenvogue.com/story/how-beauty-brands-are-profiting-off-racism
11. www.teenvogue.com/story/tarte-cosmetics-racist-meme-backlash
12. https://time.com/4671287/karlie-kloss-vogue-backlash/
13. www.teenvogue.com/story/pepsi-commercial-kendall-jenner-reaction
14. www.dazeddigital.com/beauty/body/article/45829/1/johnny-depp-dior-sauvage-campaign-pulled-after-racism-backlash
15. www.nbcnews.com/news/us-news/Black-doctor-who-tried-help-sick-passenger-claims-flight-attendants-n930096
16. www.theguardian.com/us-news/2015/nov/21/southwest-airlines-muslim-middle-eastern-passengers
17. www.buzzfeednews.com/article/amberjamieson/alaska-airlines-newark-chaos
18. www.allure.com/story/sza-sandy-sephora-shopping-security
19. https://www.nytimes.com/2018/12/28/us/black-man-kicked-out-hotel-portland.html

20. https://www.huffpost.com/entry/Black-men-speak-out-starbucks-arrest_n_5ad8809fe4b0e4d0715dc393
21. https://abc7chicago.com/society/police-report-reveals-new-details-on-naperville-buffalo-wild-wings-racist-incident/5696571/
22. www.forbes.com/sites/rachelsandler/2019/07/09/White-man-calls-police-on-Black-man-waiting-for-friend-at-san-francisco-apartment-building/#12d1915062b5
23. www.sciencedaily.com/releases/2009/03/090331091252.htm
24. www2.deloitte.com/content/dam/Deloitte/au/Documents/human-capital/deloitte-au-hc-diversity-inclusion-soup-0513.pdf
25. www.mckinsey.com/business-functions/organization/our-insights/delivering-through-diversity
26. www.bcg.com/en-us/publications/2018/how-diverse-leadership-teams-boost-innovation.aspx
27. www.directwomen.org/sites/default/files/news-pdfs/9.pdf
28. https://hbr.org/2013/12/how-diversity-can-drive-innovation
29. https://insight.kellogg.northwestern.edu/article/better_decisions_through_diversity

Chapter 4

Old Rule of Diversity #2. Make Sure You Mention That Bias Is OK

"Excuse me," I look up from pushing my toddler daughter on a swing to see the young White woman smiling at me. It's Spring 2014. I'm on a playground in my neighborhood on the North Side of Chicago. Chicago is one of the most racially segregated cities in America, and my neighborhood is, like the North Side of Chicago, predominantly White.

The woman is around my age, and she's been pushing a child on the swing as well. We've been the only two people on the playground for a while, but this is the first time she's spoken to me.

She looks at my daughter. She looks at me. "I just want to say," she starts, looking a bit uncertain. My smile falters. Then she perks up. "You take such good care of her. If I ever see her mom, I'll let her know that." She smiles at me again, takes who I had assumed to be her child (but who knows now?!) out of the swing, and walks away.

This was the first time a White mom in my neighborhood mistook me for my children's nanny. It wouldn't be the last time. Over and over again, for years and right up until the day I am typing these words, I am constantly mistaken as the nanny to my own children.

But it's not even enough that they assume that! It's the questions they ask next. "How much am I paid? Am I looking for work? Are my friends looking for work? How much do they make?" You would be shocked by how many White moms on the North Side of Chicago are trying to steal nannies! It's like the Hunger Games of nannies out here.

Now, to be fair, the Black woman from Belize who took care of my children while I worked is a lovely human being. I'm fine being called the nanny if that was the reason. But it's not the reason. I am not being called the nanny because they think I am a lovely human being. I am being called the nanny because I am Black. Those White moms look at me, see I am Black, and make an immediate assumption – I am the nanny.

That is what I call implicit or unconscious bias. It has been, by my very unscientific estimation, the starting point for almost every diversity training for companies across the world for the past decade. I'm going to give you a crash course on unconscious bias. Let's start by showing you how your brain navigates facts coming at you at lightning speed.

Two Lawyers Walk into a Bar ...

Two lawyers, partners in a law firm, walk into a local bar. Right behind them a truck driver who really wants to stop at this bar for the night. The lawyers nod at a judge in the corner, whom they know, and note that the judge is sitting with one of their legal assistants.

The lawyers go up to the bartender, the bartender asks what they would like to drink, the bartender pours the drinks, the lawyers say cheers, and they start to drink. Suddenly, one of the lawyers starts choking, falls, and is caught by the truck driver who was sitting on a neighboring stool.

The bartender calls out for a doctor. Two doctors and a firefighter rush up to the bar, as does the judge and the legal assistant. The firefighter pounds on the lawyer's back and starts to administer CPR. Finally, the lawyer starts coughing and is able to breathe again.

Everyone is extremely relieved. The lawyer, supremely grateful, offers to buy the whole group drinks.

"Don't worry about it," laughs the bartender, shaking her head at the eight women standing around the bar. "Something crazy always happens when it's ladies' night at the bar."

Time for your questions. Until that last part with the bartender, I want you to be honest. Did you assume the two law firm partners were men? What about the judge? The bartender? The firefighter? The truck driver? The doctors? What about the legal assistant? Did you assume the legal assistant was a man?

I have done this exercise with countless groups over the years. To a person, the group visualizes all of the unnamed people in the scene as men, except for the legal assistant, even in groups of primarily women.

It's not just gender. Were either of your lawyers Black? Was your truck driver Latinx? Was your bartender Native American? Again, the group generally identifies everyone in the room as White, except for the legal assistant. And perhaps a few of the background characters. The ones who don't have any speaking roles. The "help." Not the ones who drive the narrative. Those roles are reserved for White men.

See, your brain is very smart. It's your brain! It wants to categorize things. That's how unconscious bias works.

This Is Your Brain on Bias

Unconscious bias is a lens through which we view the world. It helps us to automatically filter how we take in and act on information. It's universal – everyone has it. Millions of years ago, prehistoric people faced constant threats from animals, nature, and human outsiders. They needed to make immediate life-and-death decisions about those dangers, so they evolved an unconscious system of broad categorizations. This system remains extraordinarily useful today – we wouldn't be able to go through our days without it. But that means it is also extraordinarily easy to fall into the habits that bias creates.

In 2011, Nobel Prize winner Daniel Kahneman published his best-selling book *Thinking Fast and Slow*. An expert on heuristics and cognitive biases, Kahneman wrote about two systems of the brain: System 1 and System 2. System 1 is fast, automatic, and unconscious. It makes instant conclusions about everyone and everything and controls 99% of the information coming at you. It's your brain on autopilot. System 2, by contrast, is calm, reflective, and controlled. It's rational, but it takes a while to kick in, and even when it does, it relies heavily on what System 1 is telling it. Put simply, System 1 processes the data and sends it to System 2 to analyze. But to process that data, System 1 has to rely on something else: schemas.

Schemas are patterns of thought. They are the unconscious models of reality we use to categorize the many bits of information we receive at any point in time. We form these patterns from our lived experiences, with different activities, observations, and people, and also vicariously, through impressions from stories, books, movies, media, and culture. And so, when we are asked to picture a partner at a law firm, what does our brain do? It gathers up all the information it has to inform a schema of a White man. *That* is unconscious bias.

The Many, Many Studies of Unconscious Bias

Meet Thomas Meyer,[1] a fictional associate used in a research study at a law firm. The study asked 60 law firm partners to review a memorandum – a document outlining legal arguments – that the fictional Thomas Meyer had written. Here's where it gets interesting: half the partners were told that Thomas Meyer was White, and the other half were told Thomas Meyer was Black. All 60 of those partners were asked to grade Thomas Meyer's memorandum.

The results are illuminating. The 30 partners who were told Thomas Meyer was White gave the memo an average rating of 4.1 out of 5. The 30 partners who were told Thomas Meyer was Black gave the memo an average rating of 3.2 out of 5. In addition, the "White" Thomas Meyer was praised for things like his potential and his good analytical skills, while the "Black" Thomas Meyer was criticized as average at best and needing a lot of work. As if that weren't enough, the partners also found an average of 2.9 out of 7 spelling and grammar errors in the "White" Thomas Meyer's memo, but nearly twice as many – 5.8 out of 7 – in the memo of his "Black" counterpart. They also made 11 comments on formatting for the "White" Thomas Meyer and a whopping 29 comments for the "Black" Thomas Meyer. Because when you expect someone to stumble, you won't look for ways that they succeed. You will look for ways that they stumble. Ways that they fit into your schema. Ways that they confirm your bias.

In another study, 250 fictional people with a variety of names identifiable by gender or ethnicity (e.g., Brad Anderson, Lamar Washington, Mei Chen) sent identical emails to top professors around the country, saying they were interested in their work and they would love to learn more. The researchers found that women and minorities were systematically less likely to get responses from the professors – especially Indian and Chinese students. The bias was especially profound with professors of private universities, natural science professors, and business school professors.[2]

A similar study sent identical resumes, one with the name Jennifer and one with the name John, to over 100 science professors around the country, asking them to assess the resume's quality. Despite having the same qualifications and experience as John, Jennifer was viewed as significantly less competent by the professors, who were also less willing to mentor or hire her. They also recommended paying her a lower salary – on average, $4,000 per year less than John.[3]

A different study evaluating post-doctoral applications found that women had to be two and a half times as productive as men just to be rated equally as competent.[4] And another resume study actually found that White applicants who identified as just having been released from prison received more callbacks than Black applicants *with no criminal record at all.*[5]

Here's the last one. A study found that women were 1.4 times more likely to receive critical subjective feedback on their performance reviews than were men.[6] For example, "Heidi seems to shrink when she's around clients especially. She needs to be more assertive," but "Jim needs to develop his natural ability to work with people," or "Simone seems paralyzed and confused when she's facing tight deadlines to make decisions," but "Cameron seems hesitant in making decisions, yet is able to work out multiple alternative solutions and determine the most suitable one." It's the halo effect he has because he's a man, and there's a more positive spin on his work, and the horns effect that she has because she's a woman, and there's a more negative spin around her work.

The Words We Use for Women

Let's continue diving into gender bias. An analysis of performance reviews in the military found that there were no gender differences in objective measures like grades, fitness scores, or class standings – only in subjective measures.[7] Women were assigned significantly more negative attributes than men: inept, selfish, frivolous, passive, scattered, opportunistic, gossip, excitable, vain, panicky, temperamental, and indecisive. Men, on the other hand, were only assigned two negative characteristics: arrogant and irresponsible. Now, think about when we get to the promotion level.

Which of those negative characteristics can be overcome? Which of those can be seen in a positive light? Which of those get the halo effect? Would you rather work with the arrogant commander or the inept one?

That's what makes unconscious bias so insidious. It's constantly reinforced by what we see and do in the society around us. It's how we think of men versus women, and it affects what adjectives we use to describe one that we would never use to describe the other. It's the quote in my daughter's bedroom: "No one ever calls boys bossy."

In my longer workshops on leadership, I have people split into three groups. I ask the first group to write down words typically associated with men, the second group to write down words typically associated with women, and the third group to write down words typically associated with leaders. I bet you can guess what happens. The lists of words used for men and leaders overlap considerably – strong, decisive, and confident – whereas the words used to describe women, like compassionate, empathetic, and maternal, are almost never on the list of words used for leaders.

It leads to something like this, one of my favorite tidbits of information. It's from *Blink* by Malcolm Gladwell.[8] According to Gladwell, in the U.S. population, around 14.5% of men are over 6 feet tall. But among CEOs of Fortune 500 companies, that number is 58%. The percentage of adult men over 6 feet 2 inches is 3.9%. Of Fortune 500 companies, that number is 30%.

Why do we equate height with leadership? Why does the tall kid on the playground become the leader? When does it happen? How does it happen? Here's one more thing. The average height of a woman in the United States is 5 feet 4 inches. As of this writing, there are 37 women CEOs of Fortune 500 companies.

That's bias. But now you're probably wondering why exactly I said bias was an old rule. If it is so problematic and so endemic to how we see people, then shouldn't it be exactly the kind of challenge we need to work together to overcome? It is. That's not my problem with bias. My problem with bias is how we talk about it.

Microaggressions, or the Death by a Thousand Cuts

"Bias is universal."

"Everyone has bias."

"Don't be afraid that you're biased."

"You have biases, and that's OK!"

Time after time, this is the kind of phrasing you hear around bias. It's as if we're trying to comfort a five-year-old child whose favorite toy got broken. We act like bias is just something that exists, and as long as we acknowledge that it's there, the fact that we have it isn't a real problem at all.

It means I need to tell you the truth about bias. I want to share what it feels like. How it cuts you down. How it makes you feel less than. How it tells you over and over again that you do not belong in this space at all.

It's in what we call microaggressions – the subtle verbal and non-verbal slights, the insults, the indignities, and the denigrating messages directed toward an individual because of their group membership.[9]

"Kim, can you take notes?" And it's not really a question because Kim is the only woman in the room and they always ask her to take notes.

"Oh, I'm sorry. I'm looking for the manager who's supposed to be sitting here. Have you seen him?" – he uncomfortably peeks his head into my office as I, the Black woman manager with my name on the door, am sitting right there.

"Well, that's not a real disability," she laughs at her colleague suffering from an anxiety disorder.

"Wow, your English is really good," the Chinese-American architect hears, which is surprising to him since he's been speaking English since he could talk.

"I will never be able to pronounce your name," someone shakes their head, as if mispronouncing one of the most crucial aspects of someone's identity is little more than a joke. I always love this story from actress Uzoamaka (Uzo) Aduba. After the children and teachers in her grade school class had such difficulty pronouncing her name, she went home and asked her mother if she could be called Zoe. As Aduba tells it, "I remember she was cooking, and in her Nigerian accent she said, 'Why?'" I said, "Nobody can pronounce it." Without missing a beat, she said, "If they can learn to say Tchaikovsky and Michelangelo and Dostoyevsky, they can learn to say Uzoamaka."[10]

Let's keep going. "Where does your husband work?" The married lesbian engineer gets asked, over and over again.

"You just weren't the right fit for this client," the South Asian woman is told as she's passed over for a project again. But she was the right fit for the pitch. She was the right fit for the company's marketing materials.

"Can't believe you're still doing this at your age!" the 67-year-old accountant hears on a team video call.

"Where are you from?" the Latina consultant gets asked. And when she says, "America?" she gets told with a laugh, "No, no, no. Where are you from really?"

"What are you?" People ask my biracial children all the time. And then they touch their hair. If there is only one lesson you take away from this book, please do not touch my children's hair. Don't touch anyone's hair. People are not pets. Do not pet them.

"Who's going to watch your kids while you're working?" But Kim's husband never gets asked that question. That assumption is never made about him.

"Defendants check in over there." That's what the clerk says to my friend's husband, a Black male law student at his first court hearing. He walks in and that's the first thing the clerk says when she sees him. That's the category the clerk places him into.

"He's so well-spoken," the clerk might whisper to her colleague as he walks away. I cannot tell you how many times I have been called well-spoken in my life. "So articulate!" the surprised exclamation goes. As if it is a surprise that someone who looks like me should speak the way I do. As if I am a "credit" to my race.

Then there's the alternative. "Can you not take that tone right now?" she says offended, as I am beyond calm in explaining why what she did – what she said – was wrong.

Because it's not enough that those things are said. It's the response I might get when I'm brave enough to call the speaker out on what they said. When I say, "Please don't say that," "That was wrong," "That's not at all my experience," I try to provide a teaching moment. I try to move past the discomfort. I try to engage with the misunderstanding.

But what am I told in response? "I wasn't serious." "Just get over it." "It's not a big deal." "It was just a joke." "I never said that." "Why are you blaming me?"

It's what the experts call "microinvalidations."[11] It's what I call gaslighting. You know, what really bad exes, or bad bosses, do. Telling me that what I felt, what hurt me, isn't true. If there's one thing that unconscious bias really feels like, it is experiencing these microinequities and being told you are imagining them. Or worse, that you are the problem for calling people's attention to the problem (see Gabrielle Union and *America's Got Talent*, circa 2019). That's what unconscious bias feels like. That's why saying everyone has it and that's OK simply is not enough.

How Individual Bias Leads to Institutional Bias

Unconscious bias is not an individual issue. It is not one lone wolf in the workplace, making rogue statements. It is an institutional-level problem that exists throughout organizations, top to bottom.

Consider *affinity bias*, the preference we have for people in our in-group. They look like us, went to our school, like the same sports we do, or have a similar first name. We are more inclined to think positively about them. I like me and so it naturally follows that I will like people who are like me, and I will think more positively about people who are like me than people who are not.

Here's what that looks like at the individual level. Brad comes in and he sits down for an interview. Brad is wearing clothes that I would wear; he's from a town like me; he went to a similar school as me; and when I look at Brad, I know this is someone I can hang with. Someone I can talk to and give work to. Because Brad's a good guy. And because Brad's a good guy, I am more inclined to hire Brad, even if his resume is very similar to Ibrahim, or even if his resume is very different from Ibrahim, but Brad's resume has more on it that I can relate to. The conversation flows smoother with Brad. So Brad gets the very best recommendation. Brad is the "right fit."

Then there's *attribution bias*. Think back a minute to those law firm reviews. Maybe Brad isn't your guy. But Brad and men who look like Brad have usually been The Guy. They have been The Guy in leadership; they have been The Guy in positions of power. When you search for manager or CEO in Google, or when they're typecasting for, you know, 90s superheroes, Brad is who comes up. The Guy. So Brad gets something else. Not just the "right fit." He also gets "competent." Because he's a "natural leader." When Brad does really good work, quality work, it's because he's good at his job. He's smart, he's diligent, he's hard-working, he's all those positive adjectives we use in those military reviews. It's easy to believe that Brad is good because people who look like Brad are, in every space in a majority-White world, the exemplar – in the top-grossing movies that are written and directed and starring White men, our literary heroes, our CEOs, our presidents, our senators, our judges, our congressmen, our history, our street names, our buildings, our organization names, our statues, our money. Brad, by virtue of his birth in this country, is an heir to that legacy.

But Ibrahim isn't. In the corporate America ladder that Ibrahim is trying to climb, he is often the first and the only. When his evaluators are considering interviewing or promoting him, the bias and the stereotype that they call readily to mind isn't the long history of success that people who look like Ibrahim have had, but instead the spaces where people who look like Ibrahim have been allowed into.

If they are in movies or books, they are relegated to stereotypical roles – as numerous Middle Eastern actors can tell you, it's a taxi driver or a terrorist. If they are in companies, they are often not in the C-suite or in positions of leadership. They don't have children cartoons about them. The list of 100 greatest American authors typically doesn't include people of their ethnicity. There is no positive bias that people who look like Ibrahim are competent to be in the space that he wants to be in. He is often seen as "less than" not "equal to," even if that assumption is only made unconsciously, which is why, even if they have identical resumes, Brad's resume gets the callback, and Ibrahim's does not.

And that's when attribution bias rears its ugly head. Because when Brad does something good or smart, that's because people like Brad are often competent and smart. But when Ibrahim does something competent or smart, that's because he got lucky. He had help. He managed to figure it out. Then Brad and Ibrahim both stumble. We can brush it aside because people like Brad stumble, but they get back up. Ibrahim, however? Well, it just shows that "people like him" aren't "ready," that he's "under-qualified," "unprepared," and "needs extra help." Remember Thomas Meyer? Because that's what easily fits the biased narrative that we have built our entire lives. Our brain may be smart, but as System 1 and System 2 thinking demonstrate, it's also extremely lazy.

And because I knew that Ibrahim wasn't the right fit, I'm
going to remember that time he was five minutes late for
the meeting. Or I know that people like him don't speak up
confidently so I'll make a note that he's too quiet in meetings.
He had to miss a meeting because of a family crisis, and you
know that's just going to happen again and again. That's *con-
firmation bias*, where someone's actions already confirm your
pre-conceived notion that you already had of them. Combine
that with attribution bias. Brad was running late for the meeting because he was working hard on some client matters.
Brad doesn't talk much because he's "a man of few words."
Brad has had family challenges this year, but "he manages to
keep his personal life separate from work."

All of those individual biases – affinity, attribution, con-
firmation, and many more – together combine to result in
organization-wide *institutional bias.* The bias baked into our
systems, the bias that exists in how we hire, mentor, and
promote people. Where we favor the "in-group" to the detriment of the "out-group." Where the individual biased decisions
that we make lead to repeated patterns over and over again
in groups that aren't getting mentored, groups that don't get
the good work, groups that don't get the executive coaching
to succeed, groups that aren't receiving the effective feedback,
groups that don't even make it in the door in the first place.

What questions do we ask in interviews? (Are we just looking for the right fit?) What factors are most favorable in promotions? (Who was able to work long hours and late nights and
give me the facetime I needed?) What schools do we recruit
at? (There are really only four schools we should be looking
at; they happen to be the same four schools that our founders
attended.) How do we obtain work? (Individual competition is
best; the cream will rise to the top!) How do we deliver feedback? (We don't need constant cheerleading; twice a year is
enough for us.) How do we staff projects? (This isn't elemen-
tary school; not everyone gets a chance.) Institutional bias
rises again and again when our organizational systems ensure

that one group, typically the one that designed the systems to reflect the values they prioritize, keeps on getting ahead.

That's bias. You don't need to remember the names. There is no test after you've finished this book. What I want you to remember, to really remember, is how bias works to keep fully qualified people from success.

That's why I want us to get real on bias. Because the old rule of saying it's OK and everyone has it does a serious injustice to the people who are struggling with the effects of it every day – the emotional toll, the physical toll, and the career toll it takes. So please toss that old rule out of the door and recognize that bias really is the death by a thousand cuts, and it is causing the minorities in your workplaces to suffer in place, one deep cut at a time.

Notes

1. http://nextions.com/wp-content/uploads/2017/05/written-in-Black-and-White-yellow-paper-series.pdf
2. www.npr.org/2014/04/22/305814367/evidence-of-racial-gender-biases-found-in-faculty-mentoring
3. www.pnas.org/content/109/41/16474
4. www.nature.com/articles/387341a0
5. https://scholar.harvard.edu/files/pager/files/pager_ajs.pdf
6. https://hbr.org/2017/04/how-gender-bias-corrupts-performance-reviews-and-what-to-do-about-it
7. https://hbr.org/2018/05/the-different-words-we-use-to-describe-male-and-female-leaders
8. Gladwell, Malcolm. *Blink: The Power of Thinking without Thinking*. New York: Little, Brown And Co., 2005. Print.
9. Sue, Derald Wing. *Microaggressions in Everyday Life: Race, Gender, and Sexual Orientation*, 1st Edition.
10. www.improper.com/arts-culture/the-eyes-have-it/
11. Derald Wing Sue, author of the 2010 book, *Microaggressions in Everyday Life*.

Chapter 5

Old Rule of Diversity #3. Whatever You Do, Don't Mention Race

Back to my story. You might remember that in the years after I left law firm life, I traveled around the state of Illinois speaking about civility, professionalism, and diversity. During those years, I talked about bias quite a lot. I attended a number of bias presentations, bias discussions, bias strategy sessions, and on and on and on. Unconscious bias is big business for a lot of organizations and for good reason; how we treat others and the groups in which we place them has a lot to do with success and failure in the professional world.

When I spoke about bias, I would tell people the nanny story from earlier. It was then, and still is, remarkably effective. I would then talk about how the brain works, how stereotypes work, and how they affect our perception of others. I would talk about how we interrupt it, what strategies we can put into place, what systems to leverage, how to rewire our brains. In the 2010s, unconscious bias was THE topic of conversation in diversity. Addressing it was THE solution.

Until the day I went home early after a speech. My children's nanny was there, as I shared earlier, a young Black woman from Belize. I sat down with her. We caught up on our days. As I told her about the program I had done earlier, I realized that I had never actually told her the story of the White moms in this neighborhood calling me the nanny. I wondered what her reaction would be. Would she think it funny? Strange? Would she be offended? I didn't know, but I had been telling a story that, in a way, belonged to her as well. I wanted to know what she thought.

I told her the story. She laughed. But then she said something else, something that I have never forgotten:

"Michelle, that's when they talk to you. Most of the time, they don't even bother talking to us."

I stopped short. Because that's the missing piece of the story. She was right. Most of the time, they didn't say anything to you at all, if they're White and you're Black. They don't look you in the eye. They don't sit next to you on the bench. They don't include you in their conversations. They treat you like a stranger who doesn't belong, who doesn't fit.

And that right there is Old Rule #3. It's what we don't talk about, heck what we actively try to avoid when we label something "bias."

Unconscious bias tells you a lot. It tells you that you have biases, it tells you where those biases come from, and it tells you how to be aware of them. Unconscious bias trainings that stay on Old Rule #2 will tell you how to structure around them, how to use strategies, and how to interrupt them. But you know what unconscious bias doesn't tell you? It doesn't tell you why these biases are wrong; it doesn't tell you why you think the way you do, and it doesn't tell you how to end it. Not biases; you can't end bias. But rather, how do you end the reason you believe that bias in the first place? The old rules say we shouldn't mention that reason. The old rules say we shouldn't even speak that word. Instead, we should say that we all have biases and that's okay.

The old rules need to change.

"You're Supposed to Pretend You Don't Notice Certain Things"

To help us change the old rules, I turn to the work of another Black woman immigrant, Chimanada Ngozi Adichie and her 2013 novel, *Americanah*. If you haven't read *Americanah*, please do. Not only because it is an excellent book, but also because I look forward to the day in my lifetime when Chimanada Ngozi Adichie becomes the first Black African woman to win the Nobel Prize for Literature.

Americanah is the story of a young Nigerian woman named Ifemelu who comes to America to attend school. She is Black and when the story starts, she's at a place near and dear to my heart, Princeton University. It's the reason that 17-year-old Michelle also came to America. The book is all about Ifemelu and her life in America then back in Nigeria. One of the vignettes Adichie tells in the book is about Ifemelu, her Nigerian friend, Ginika, and their experience in America buying a dress.

Picture a store. (Adichie doesn't specify what store in her book, but with its loud music, dim lighting, and attractive salespeople, I always picture Abercrombie & Fitch.) There are three women sales clerks in the store – one at the register and two on the floor. Of the two on the floor, one sales clerk is Black and one is White. The White sales clerk helps the women find a dress.

At the register, the cashier, who is White, asks Ginika which of the clerks helped them. Ginika looks around; she doesn't see either woman on the floor, and she doesn't know either of their names. Here is Adichie's description of the scene that follows:[1]

> "Was it the one with long hair?" the cashier asked.
> "Well, both of them have long hair."
> "The one with dark hair?"
> Both of them had dark hair.

Ginika smiled and looked at the cashier, and the cashier smiled and she looked at her computer screen, and two damp seconds crawled past before she cheerfully said, "It's okay, I'll figure it out later and make sure she gets her commission."

As they walked out of the store, Ifemelu said, "I was waiting for her to ask, 'Was it the one with two eyes or the one with two legs?' Why didn't she just ask, 'Was it the black girl or the white girl?'" Ginika laughed. "Because this is America. You're supposed to pretend that you don't notice certain things."

_____

That conversation is at the heart of Old Rule #3. Those White moms at the playground may think I'm the nanny because of unconscious bias, but their decision not to talk to me or to my children's nanny is not unconscious – any more than it is an unconscious decision to call the police on Black people who are barbecuing in a park, selling water on the street, standing in a hotel lobby, dancing on the beach, shopping in a makeup store, or sitting in a coffee shop.

That decision is all about race. Race, race, race, race, race. Race is the "thing" that Ginika rightly points out we pretend not to notice in America. But here, I'll be blunter than Adichie was: It is predominantly White America that pretends this. Many White Americans simply do not like talking about race, and many White Americans especially do not like using race to explain bias or exclusion.

How White Americans Avoid Talking about Race

Here's how those White moms might answer to the charge that they don't talk to me or my nanny: "We don't have anything in common. Yes, she has kids and I have kids, but it's not the same thing. I mean, she's probably not even from this neighborhood. Plus, she wouldn't want to talk to me anyway."

Yes, it's the same reason I didn't sit next to the Black kids at lunch. Because we didn't have anything in common. I'm not friends with the Black guy at work because we don't have anything in common. I didn't have any Black roommates, or Black college friends or there weren't any Black women in my bridal party, and no, I don't have any Black neighbors but no, no, no, it's not because of race. Stop talking about race! *It has nothing to do with race!*

For their entire lives, White Americans like the cashier in *Americanah* have been socialized to believe that the color of one's skin makes no difference at all, and that to even mention it makes them look like racists. It's those who point out the differences that are the problem, not those who ignore them.

See Americans, and again to be specific, mainly White Americans, work so hard to be like that cashier in *Americanah*. Many try to find all other explanations except the one that the country in which we all live is the simplest, most obvious one of all – that it has everything to do with race. As Eduardo Bonilla-Silva explains in his excellent book, *Racism without Racists*, those in denial about the centrality of race will create this extraordinarily elaborate narrative as to why different outcomes occur that have nothing to do with race. Because, as he says in the very title of his book, White Americans work so hard to be one thing in this country – colorblind.[2]

"I don't see race," they proudly proclaim, or "I don't see color."

"I am the least racist person in the world!"

"We are all one race – the human race."

"I voted for Obama."

"Race won't even matter in 50 years."

"Did you forget what Dr. King said? It's about the content of the character, not the color of the skin!"

So goes America, so goes the workplace. Many of the White leaders with whom I work start out like that cashier in *Americanah*. They try not to see race. They grab at every other explanation under the sun for their deplorable diversity numbers. They call it merit. They call it coincidence. They call it, "We just didn't have anything in common." They call it, "She didn't lean in." They just don't call it race.

How hard is it for White Americans to talk about race? You might remember the game, "Guess Who?" If you don't, here's how Guess Who works. You and your opponent have two boards with the same pictures of faces facing each of you. Each of you then has a card in front of you with one of those pictures. Your goal is to guess which picture your opponent has by narrowing down the pictures on the board, which means you ask questions like, "Does your person have brown eyes?" "Is your person wearing a hat?" "Does your person have blonde hair?" You want to use as few questions as possible to win.

Fast forward to 2006. Researchers created a new version of Guess Who.[3] Instead of the classic Guess Who board, they made a very different board. This board had 12 pictures of faces on it. Half of the pictures were White faces, half of the pictures were Black faces, and the 30 White testers had to play Guess Who with it.

Now, I talk about race all the time. I also really like to win games. So if I were looking at this board, the first question I would ask is, "Is your person Black?" But that's not what the White participants did. Only 57% of those who played with a White opponent used the word "Black" or "African-American." Even worse, when the White participants played against a Black opponent, only 21% of those White players asked whether the opposing player's picture was Black. And when they did ask the question, they looked nervous, uncomfortable, and anxious. Why? Because they were worried that they would appear racist. But here's an interesting tidbit about the test. When the researchers brought in observers to determine which of the questioners appeared more biased – the ones who asked about race versus the ones who did not – the observers found the questioners who avoided the race question far more biased than the ones who asked.

You know who did much better at this test? Third graders. But you know who did just as badly? Fourth and fifth graders. That colorblind approach, that recognition that you can't talk about racial differences, it starts as early as age 10.

Which means the next study shouldn't surprise anyone. In the 2009 book *NurtureShock*, authors Ashley Merryman and Po Bronson describe a study by researcher Birgitte Vittrup on whether videos with multicultural storylines had a beneficial effect on children's understanding of race. As part of the study, Vittrup asked one group of parents to talk with their children five nights per week on issues of race. Here's what happened next. It's a long quote, but please read it all.

> Five families in [the] group abruptly quit the study. Two directly told Vittrup, "We don't want to have these conversations with our child. We don't want to point out skin color." Vittrup was taken aback— these families volunteered knowing full well it was a study of children's racial attitudes. Yet once they were aware that the study required talking openly about race, they started dropping out. [A]ccording to Vittrup's entry surveys, hardly any of these White parents had ever talked to their children directly about race. They might have asserted vague prin-ciples – like "Everybody's equal" or "God made all of us" or "Under the skin, we're all the same" – but they'd almost never called attention to racial differ-ences. They wanted their children to grow up color-blind. But Vittrup's first test of the kids revealed they weren't colorblind at all. Asked how many white peo-ple are mean, these children commonly answered, "Almost none." Asked how many blacks are mean, many answered, "Some," or "A lot." More disturbing, Vittrup also asked all the kids a very blunt question: "Do your parents like black people?" Fourteen per-cent said outright, "No, my parents don't like black

people"; 38% of the kids answered, "I don't know."
In this supposed race-free vacuum being created
by parents, kids were left to improvise their own
conclusions.

So it begins, and so it continues for the rest of those children's
lives.

What Are the Colors of Your World?

This is why it's time to be honest. If you are a White person
reading this book, you firmly believe that you are colorblind,
and you do not make any judgments based on race, with
whom you socialize, where you choose to live, or with whom
you choose to work, then I would like you to answer a few
questions for me, if you have answers for them:

What was the race of your four best friends when you were
    nine?
When you were 19?
When you were 39?
What about your first boss?
Your last boss?
Your first crush?
Your first mentor?
Your favorite college professor?
Your dentist?
Your neighborhood?
Your closest neighbor?
Your significant other?
What's the predominant race in your kid's school?
What race is your kid's best friend?
What about your child's favorite author?
Your child's favorite teacher?

Your child's coach?
Your favorite author?
The star of your favorite movie?
The mayor of your town?
Your doctor?
Your senator?
Your president?

As I've mentioned before, my children are biracial, and we are members of an online community that connects multiracial families across the Chicagoland area. I heard about the above exercise from a transracial adoptive family. Transracial adoptive families are parents, typically White, who adopt children of a different race or ethnicity from them. This exercise is one several adoption agencies do. The reason they do it is simple: if all the people your children see in your world are White like you – all the lawyers, the doctors, the accountants, the celebrities, the musicians, the teachers, the authors, the coworkers, the friends – then what will they think of their own race? What will they think of their own identity? When will they realize that you don't believe that their race is as worthy as your own?

Quick, if you are a White person, name 10 people of color you are friends with. Not on social media but in real life. If it's hard to do, know that you are not alone: in America, the average White person has 91 White friends and 9 friends of color – including just one Black friend.[4] Seventy-five percent of White Americans *have no friends of color at all.* When White people have no peers of color outside the workplace, they often don't have peers of color inside the workplace either. They don't hire them, refer them, promote them, or mentor them. That's why pretending that we don't notice race needs to stay in the past where it belongs. Instead, we need to reckon with that past, and what that means for our present.

This is Our Nation on Systemic Racism

Often I get asked by White parents, "How do I talk to my kids about race?" When they ask me, "how to talk about race," it is always shorthand for them wanting to know how to talk to their kids about Black people in America.

First, I acknowledge that I am the wrong person to ask that question. My 7-year-old routinely stands in our front yard and yells at perfect strangers, "My mom is Black! Do you like Black people?" Second, I say that your children have been noticing race since they were babies, and they have been noticing that you *don't* talk about race since they were 10. But most of all, I say this. Kids don't listen to what you say. They look at how you live.

That means reckoning with truths. The truths about the choices your parents made, their parents made, the choices you make, the choices you may be making for your children, how very much centered on race those choices are. That as much as you would like to say, "I don't see race," and "I don't see color," that the truth about your life demonstrates that you very much see race. You very much see the color of someone's skin. It's only once you reckon with it, that you can start to change it.

If you are White, you are the beneficiary of the many ways that this nation has been structured to benefit Whiteness to the detriment of those who are not White. This is what we call systemic racism. I said at the start of this book that I would be specific about the lens through which I see. Racism, that awful combination of prejudice plus power, is inflicted against every non-White racial group in America. Here, however, I am going to talk about systemic racism in terms of Black and White.

If you want to talk with your kids, friends, relatives, or yourself, about what it means to be Black, in a country that has been structured to privilege Whiteness since the first slaves arrived in bondage in 1619, I need you to also reckon with what it has meant in this country to be White. I need you to reckon with your Whiteness before you reckon with my Blackness.

To reckon with Whiteness, is to acknowledge that we call them plantations instead of slave labor camps (and we have weddings on them!), that Wall Street was one of the largest slave markets in America, and that Phillip Reid was the name of the slave who built the Statue of Freedom on top of the U.S. Capitol.[5]

To reckon with Whiteness, is to acknowledge that White families were given federally backed mortgages to buy houses while Black families were denied the same. We call it redlining.[6]

To reckon with Whiteness, is to acknowledge that instead of a GI Bill, a Black hero returns from World War II and is beaten and blinded by a White police chief for wanting to take a bathroom break. His name was Sergeant Isaac Woodard.[7]

To reckon with Whiteness, is to acknowledge that predominantly White K–12 schools receive $23 billion dollars more in funding than schools that serve students of color.[8]

To reckon with Whiteness, is to acknowledge that for similar crimes, Black men are sentenced to 20% longer prison terms than their fellow White citizens.[9]

To reckon with Whiteness, is to acknowledge that the median White household has about $171,000 in wealth to the median Black household's $17,000.[10]

To reckon with Whiteness, is to acknowledge that 24 states in America have an an all-White Supreme Court bench, including 8 states with predominantly minority populations.[11]

To reckon with Whiteness, is to acknowledge that 1 in 3 Black men born in 2001 will go to prison in their lifetimes.[12]

To reckon with Whiteness, is to acknowledge that a White couple is seen as finding supplies in the middle of Hurricane Katrina but a Black man is seen as looting.[13]

To reckon with Whiteness, is to acknowledge that in a city like Baltimore, "for every dollar spent on police, 55 cents is spent on schools, 5 cents is spent on the city's jobs programs, and a penny is spent on mental health services and violence prevention."[14]

To reckon with Whiteness, is to acknowledge that Black women are 3.2 times more likely to die in childbirth than White women.[15]

To reckon with Whiteness, is to acknowledge the Supreme Court holdings that make it as easy to suppress a Black vote in 2020 as it was in 1960 when a Black man was asked to count the bumps on a cucumber so he could cast his right as a U.S. citizen to vote.[16]

To reckon with Whiteness, is to acknowledge the enormous student debt loads that Black Americans carry as compared to their White counterparts.[17]

To reckon with Whiteness, is to acknowledge that the percentage of Black people owning a house in America has not shifted since 1968.[18]

To reckon with Whiteness, is to acknowledge that it will take a Black woman an extra four and a half months to be paid the same as a White woman.[19]

To reckon with Whiteness, is to acknowledge that of the already abysmal 37 women CEOs of Fortune 500 companies, not a single one of them is Black.[20]

To reckon with Whiteness, is to acknowledge that a Black woman who starts in an organization as a hopeful and ambitious 22-year-old, no matter how hard *she* tries, no matter how much *she* leans in, has almost zero chance of getting anywhere near that C-suite.

Systemic racism. To reckon with those words, is to acknowledge that system on top of system on top of system in this country supported by legislations, policies, regulations and rules, have denied Black people in this country from their equal claim to citizenship – inside and outside the workplace. That is the truth with which every White person in America needs to reckon. This is what it means to reckon with Whiteness.

Let's Get Honest About Race

"You're supposed to pretend that you don't notice certain things" is the old rule that needs to be abandoned. Instead, let's get honest about race. Let's get honest about why we believe some people are capable of succeeding and others are not based on the color of their skin. Let's get honest about who we choose as our peers and who we choose to be around in the workplace. Let's get honest about who we see as competent to do the work and who we do not. Let's get honest about our diversity numbers. Let's get honest and say out loud that the reason Jasmine did not succeed is because she is Black. And because she is Black, the microaggressions, the exclusions, the isolation, the demand for perfection, the withholding of second chances, the extra work she carries, the sheer discomfort a White male feels when asking her out to lunch – all of that created an almost 0% chance that she was ever going to move up.

Getting honest about race means saying that our diversity numbers are not a coincidence. Getting honest about race means saying that our diversity numbers aren't because we don't have anything in common. Getting honest about race means saying out loud that we may make unconscious decisions everyday, but, like those White moms on the playground, we follow those up with very conscious choices based on race.

If you want to do the hard work of leading real diversity in your workplace, then please do the honest work of looking in the mirror and seeing what inclusion looks like in your own world. And if at the end, when you look at the ten business books you have in your office, the nine bosses you have had in your life, the eight department heads in your organization, the seven work friends you would ask out for lunch, the six mentors who you could email right now for advice, the last five team members who were promoted, the four people you would sit next to at the company retreat, the three colleagues you would call when you land that long-sought promotion, the two people you would always staff on your team, the one person who you want to inherit your business and carry on your legacy – when you look at all this and you realize that your professional world rests on race as heavily as your personal world does, realize something else: that as a White person, you have made a choice. Please recognize that because it's only once you do that you can choose to change it.

Because what's the opposite of colorblindness? It's seeing all the colors, including your own. When a White child says to you, "Oh, that boy's skin is so dark," don't say to her, "Shh, don't say that!" Instead, tell her why his skin is dark, and please tell her why her skin is not. White is not the default. White is not everyone's "nude," "flesh-colored," or "skin-tone." White is not the norm, nor the ideal, which is precisely what racist colorblind ideology tries to tell you it is.

Ignoring the color of someone's skin does not make you colorblind. The color of my skin matters a whole lot to me. It defines my past, my present, and my future. It is my culture, it is my ancestry, it is my stamp of survival, and it is my legacy to my children. It excludes me from places I would otherwise be welcome, and it includes me in places that feel like home.

My race matters. It matters to me, it matters to you, it certainly matters in this nation. You want to judge people by the content of their character? So do I. But first, do me this favor: acknowledge that you still judge them by the color of their skin.

Notes

1. Adichie, Chimamanda Ngozi. Americanah. First edition. New York: Alfred A. Knopf, 2013., p. 77.
2. Bonilla-Silva, Eduardo, *Racism Without Racists: Color-blind Racism And The Persistence Of Racial Inequality In The United States*. Lanham, Md. : Rowman & Littlefield, 2003. p. 74.

3. www.apa.org/pubs/journals/releases/psp954918.pdf
4. www.washingtonpost.com/news/wonk/wp/2014/08/25/three-quarters-of-Whites-dont-have-any-non-White-friends/
5. https://www.businessinsider.com/american-landmarks-that-were-built-by-slaves-2019-9
6. https://www.nytimes.com/2017/08/24/upshot/how-redlinings-racist-effects-lasted-for-decades.html
7. https://www.nytimes.com/2019/02/08/us/sergeant-woodard-batesburg-south-carolina.html
8. https://www.npr.org/2019/02/26/696794821/why-white-school-districts-have-so-much-more-money
9. https://www.aclu.org/sites/default/files/assets/141027_iachr_racial_disparities_aclu_submission_0.pdf
10. https://www.pewresearch.org/fact-tank/2017/11/01/how-wealth-inequality-has-changed-in-the-u-s-since-the-great-recession-by-race-ethnicity-and-income/
11. https://www.brennancenter.org/our-work/research-reports/state-supreme-court-diversity
12. https://www.sentencingproject.org/criminal-justice-facts/
13. https://www.latimes.com/nation/la-na-harvey-20170829-story.html
14. https://labornotes.org/2020/06/its-way-past-time-redistribute-obscene-police-budgets-schools-hospitals-and-buses
15. https://www.cdc.gov/media/releases/2019/p0905-racial-ethnic-disparities-pregnancy-deaths.html
16. https://www.brennancenter.org/our-work/research-reports/new-voter-suppression
17. https://www.brookings.edu/research/black-white-disparity-in-student-loan-debt-more-than-triples-after-graduation/
18. https://www.washingtonpost.com/news/get-there/wp/2018/04/05/black-homeownership-is-as-low-as-it-was-when-housing-discrimination-was-legal/
19. https://en.wikipedia.org/wiki/Equal_Pay_Day
20. https://fortune.com/2017/09/27/black-female-ceos-fortune-500-companies/

Chapter 6

Old Rule of Diversity #4. Everyone Starts at the Same Starting Line

It's February 2002. I'm a sophomore at Princeton University. Then, as now, Princeton has 11 "eating clubs" – part dining hall, part social club. The eating clubs aren't officially affiliated with the university – each is privately owned. But joining an eating club is as sacred a Princeton tradition as you can find. There's a catch: it costs $10,000.

Now, when you're a 19-year-old on a scholarship, finding $10,000 is about as unlikely as finding yourself on a trip to the moon. In fact, when I called my mother, who had moved to Gaborone, Botswana, in part to pay for me to go to Princeton, her response was simple: she hung up the phone.

So it's February 2002. I think I have to join an eating club because that's what you're supposed to do, right? I have no idea where I was going to get $10,000 from. It wasn't covered under financial aid. Some magical loan fairy perhaps that offered loans to international students with no credit, collateral, or co-signers. But I think to myself, "This is a tradition and I am a terrible cook, so let's go."

I visited one of the eating clubs. It was a red brick antebellum mansion straight out of central casting from *Gone with the Wind*. I sat down in a room full of White students talking about the expensive winter vacations they had just returned from, the shopping they would do, the restaurants in New York City they recommend, the parties and the kegstands, and on and on. As the afternoon wore on, I got the sinking realization that, in a school where I had happily found my space, this was one space where I did not belong – not there, not at the other, more competitive clubs where you had to pass an Olympic-sized endurance test to even be considered. In the end, I entered the rooming lottery for a dorm with a basement kitchen and survived happily on ramen noodles and mashed potatoes for two years.

Four jobs, three cities, two kids, and 20 years later, here's what I wish I had told my 19-year-old self: *find that impossible $10,000*. Stake your place in a space where you will feel isolated and unwelcome – because that is the room where it happens. Inside that club are future CEOs, directors, managers, and senators. Outside of it are club alumni running consulting companies, hedge funds, startups, movie studios, political campaigns, and nonprofit boards – people who would serve as mentors, as introducers, and as networkers simply because you were in the same club as them. I wish I had known back then what many White parents, and some parents of color, tell their children: you have access to a more privileged space in an already-privileged space. Pay to play, and you move the starting line of your career way ahead.

Old Rule #4 is the idea that our country is a perfect meritocracy where everybody starts at the same starting line. We onboard new workers in a one-week orientation, and they're off to the races where everyone has an equal chance to win.

Excuse my language, but what absolute bullshit that is.

Jasmine and the First Generation

Do you know what it really feels like to be the first? To be the first in your family to go to college, the first to have student loans, or the first to have a job that you've only ever seen White people have on television?

Jasmine knows. Because Jasmine *was* the first in her family to go to college. And because she was the first, she has no idea what the unwritten rules of the workplace are. She was 22 years old before she walked into a skyscraper for the first time. It was when she had her interview at Devlin. She starts at Devlin, does the week of onboarding, learns how to use the email client, log her hours, write copy, draft a document, or categorize a lead.

But because she is the first, she doesn't know that in this industry, as in most, success is as much about who you know as what you do. Jasmine doesn't know who the influencers are, what the good work is, when she should stay late, what social events she should go to, what fundraisers are most important, what boards the movers and shakers are on, and so on. They don't cover any of that during orientation week.

Plus, she has all these questions that she doesn't know who to ask. What is a neat martini? What are health clubs? How much do I tip? Why does everyone own the same thousand-dollar purse? What is a good suit? She goes into the women's meeting, and they're all talking about childcare, when she just needs to know how people can think of her as competent.

You know who has that manual? Dave. It's in his DNA. Perhaps because Dave's parents worked for companies similar to Devlin. Or because Dave's father was in the same frater-nity as one of Devlin's top salesmen. Because all of Dave's aunts and uncles graduated from college and went to work for large organizations. A few of them even started their own companies. Because Dave has cousins and siblings who have already started working and given him advice on how to suc-ceed. Because Dave was seven years old when he entered a skyscraper for the first time to visit his mom at work. Because Dave has seen his parents go out to dinner with the boss, attend holiday parties, run nonprofit boards, and invite out-of-town employees home for dinner. Because Dave has overheard his mother negotiating deals on the phone. Because Dave has listened to his father talk about the next year's budget while driving to Florida for vacation. Because even if Dave had decided to spend a year after graduation lying on his parents' couch watching *Days of Our Lives*, he would still start out his working life as an heir to this legacy. He would still start that race far ahead of Jasmine.

Plus, there is still bias. There is still race. Even if Dave is as much a first-generation employee as Jasmine is, he still has the advantage in a predominantly White workplace, of being White.

And they're off. Dave is already 20 feet ahead, and his lead only grows wider and wider. Meanwhile, Jasmine is just trying to keep up. But then slowly, she realizes that something else is slowing her down: her feet seem to be stuck. She looks down. It's thick, viscous mud, and it's tripping her up. That mud is made up of *stereotype threat* and *impostor syndrome*.

What Stereotype Do You Have of Me?

The idea of stereotype threat originated in 1995 with researchers Claude Steele and Joshua Aronson. Stereotype threat happens when people enter a situation where they feel at risk of conforming to stereotypes about their social group. They become anxious about their performance and fail to perform to their full potential. Even if someone doesn't ascribe to the stereotype, they will feel stress knowing that others believe that stereotype about them, particularly in situations where that stereotype is relevant. As researchers Loriann Roberson and Carol T. Kulik note, "Every employee walking through the door of the organization knows the stereotypes that might be applied to him or her and wonders whether organizational decision makers and co-workers will endorse those stereotypes."[1]

Here's a practical example. Researchers divided participants into different groups of three – three women, two women and one man, and one woman and two men – then asked them to complete math exercises. In the two groups that included men, the women performed far worse than the women in the all-women group did.[2] Another example: when researchers described a golf game as a test of natural athletic ability, Black students performed better than White students. But when researchers described the exact same game as a test of sports intelligence, White students performed better than Black students.[3] It's a similar finding to what Steele and Aronson found when they did their seminal study on stereotype threat and told one group of students that the test was for intelligence but told the other two groups of students that this exact same test was simply a challenging verbal test. Black students did worse when they believed the test was for their intelligence but far better when they believed the test was for verbal problem-solving skills.[4] Why? Because in America, there is an ugly, negative stereotype about Black people and intelligence. The students had internalized that negative stereotype. The same stereotype does not exist about Black people and athletic ability or Black people and verbal problem-solving skills.

Where does stereotype threat leave Jasmine? She doesn't take on the high-risk assignments because she's worried that if she struggles or fails, it would reinforce the stereotype that already exists about her lack of competence. She frets in her interview when asked about her background, which makes her come across as fake and stilted instead. She's anxious in her performance reviews and tries to cover it up by projecting indifference. She overcompensates again and again to make up for a stereotype over which she has no control. That's half of the mud that keeps slowing her down.

I Feel Like a Fraud Here

Stereotype threat has a twin called impostor syndrome. If you've felt it, you know exactly what I'm talking about – the feeling that no matter how successful you are, you are a fraud, not skilled enough for the career you've chosen; that you don't deserve the success you have, it was all luck or timing, and one day someone will find out and expose you for the impostor you truly are.

That's impostor syndrome. And it's slowing Jasmine the hell down.

Impostor syndrome is in little phrases like "I'm not good enough," "I'm not smart enough," "I'm not talented enough," and "I don't know enough." People with impostor syndrome consistently compare themselves to others and find themselves falling short. They don't raise their hands. They don't accept compliments. They don't feel like they're important enough to talk to someone. They worry about asking for help because then they know people will find out they don't know what they're doing. They rewrite the same perfectly fine email over and over and over again. They are their own worst critics. And every day they come into work, they think to themselves, "Today is the day I quit for good."

Statistics suggest that 70% of Americans struggle with impostor syndrome,[5] but when it comes to minorities in the workplace, I think that number is closer to 100%. Because we are in a space that tells us again and again that we are impostors here. That we aren't good enough. That we aren't competent enough. That we really did only get here because someone overlooked a fault on our resume or decided to give us an extra push. And we look around and see that our cultures aren't represented and that our way of experiencing the world isn't validated – the first LGBTQ+ woman to work in this department, the only Sikh man on the floor. And when we find ourselves not considered for the "good work," socially isolated in the workplace, and having our competence implicitly or explicitly questioned, we start to believe that false narrative about ourselves. There might be a space for us, but that space isn't here.

The weight of being alone is exactly what faces your marginalized professionals at the starting line. And many of them, without the resources and connections inside or outside the workplace, need much more than an onboarding orientation to situate them for success.

This means you as a leader need to understand the truth that some employees have access to and knowledge of systems inside and outside of your organization that allow them a greater chance of success than others have. And in this day and age, we call that advantage something else. We call it "privilege."

The Starting Line of Privilege

Put simply, privilege is the bundle of benefits granted to someone because of who they are. If you have a minute, search on YouTube for one of the many "privilege walk" or "privilege run" videos out there. Participants line up horizontally and then are asked to step forward or backward as they answer "yes" or "no" to a series of questions assessing their relative privilege (e.g., "Did you have books in your house?" "Did one of your parents go to college?" "Did you have a vacation house?" "Did your family own your home?" "Is English your first language?" "Were your ancestors forced to come to the United States?" "Do you have a disability?"). When the questioning is over, some participants are out way in front of the others and some are way behind depending on their level of privilege – whether it's the privilege of class, ability, age, ethnicity, immigration status, or being White.

Privilege – or lack of it – is why we don't all start at the same starting line in the workplace. Privilege is feeling comfortable walking into a colonial mansion to join a 200-year-old tradition. Privilege is having $10,000 available to pay for a year of food. Privilege is having parents under-stand the importance of having those social networks when you're older. Privilege is knowing where to shop for your first day of work outfit. Privilege is knowing who to tip at hotels and how much. Privilege is going on vacations out of the country as a child. Privilege is having jewelry handed down from your mother. Privilege is not having someone second-guess your knowledge when you sit down in a room. Privilege is having a stay-at-home spouse. Privilege is knowing what knife and fork to use at the department dinner. Privilege is attending Princeton. Privilege is using Chanel No. 5. Privilege is knowing there is no stereotype that exists about you that would affect someone's percep-tion of your work.

And, for Dave and Brad and the millions of men like Dave and Brad, privilege is being a White man working in an organization where the CEO is a White man, the major-ity of the managers and directors are White men, the major-ity of promotions are White men, all the previous CEOs were White men, the next CEO will be a White man, who no one questions whether he was qualified or just an affir-mative action hire, and when a White man walks in the door, the color of his skin is never going to be the reason he feels out of place. That is both the privilege of being male and being White.

See, White privilege is working hard to find somewhere in America that your skin color makes you feel unwelcome, a place that you cannot easily leave. White privilege is the abil-ity to easily leave that place and spend every hour of every day where people who look like you are always the majority. A place where you belong. White privilege is why no mat-ter how fast a Black woman like Jasmine runs, she will never catch up on her own. White privilege is why we do not start at the same starting line. Show me an onboarding program that focuses on that, and I'll show you an organization that's ready to change the world.

Notes

1. Roberson, L., & Kulik, C.T. (May 2007). "Stereotype threat at work." *Academy of Management Perspectives, 21*(2): 24–40.
2. Inzlicht. M., Ben-Zeev, T. (September 2000). "A threatening intellectual environment: why females are susceptible to experiencing problem-solving deficits in the presence of males." *Psychological Science, 11*(5): 365–71. doi:10.1111/1467-9280.00272.
3. Stone, J., Lynch, C.I., Sjomeling, M., Darley, J.M. (1999). "Stereotype threat effects on Black and White athletic performance." *Journal of Personality and Social Psychology, 77*(6): 1213–1227. doi:10.1037/0022-3514.77.6.1213
4. Steele, Claude. *Whistling Vivaldi: And Other Clues to How Stereotypes Affect Us*. New York :W.W. Norton & Company, 2010.
5. https://so06.tci-thaijo.org/index.php/IJBS/article/view/521

Chapter 7

Old Rule of Diversity #5. And Our Culture Welcomes Everyone

"I have to tell you something."

I pause in the middle of lifting my teacup to my mouth. In my experience, starting a conversation with "I have to tell you something" usually ends badly.

The maker of the "I have to tell you something" statement is a good friend of mine from school, a White man. We had met for coffee earlier that afternoon, on a break from our jobs, to catch up on our lives and the work we do. Jasmine had been on my mind lately and I talked with him about her and what she had said to me. He listened. Then after a moment of silence, he declares his need to tell me something. I put my teacup down. Whatever bombshell he's about to impart, I want to be ready.

He takes a deep breath then blurts out. "It's easier to be Black in this country than White."

Thank goodness I put my tea down because I would have spat it out, right in his face. "Whaaaa?" "Who?" "How?" "Huh?"

I started and stopped words in my head. Finally, I look at this man and the only verbalization I could make was, "Gahhh?"

I mean, where would I start with him? I'd have to start with slavery and go all the way to Wakanda.

He sees my face. We've been friends for a while, so he knows, my dark brown skin doesn't go pale unless there's a serious disturbance in the Force. He blanches too and then quickly backtracks. "No, no, no, it's not that. It's just," he says, running a frustrated hand over his head. "It's so easy if you're *him*."

Who is this mythological "him" you might ask? That him is who I call Kevin from Yale.

"Have You Met Kevin? He Went to Yale"

Everyone knows a Kevin from Yale. Kevin from Yale is the reason that many Americans could believe for years that we lived in a post-racial society. Replace Kevin from Yale with Barack from Chicago or Colin from the South Bronx or Corey from New Jersey, and you see what I mean.

Kevin from Yale is the star athlete, top of his class, prom king, class president, Rhodes scholar, superstar intern who soared to the top – and because he is Black, it seems he has the world at his feet. He's that Black friend in the 90s teen movies, just so much cooler than everyone else. And, man, it is *so* easy to be Kevin from Yale. He's charming, he's handsome, he's chill, and he can hang with anyone. Every door is wide open for him. Kevin from Yale doesn't need affirmative action; he'd get in anyway. "It doesn't matter that he's Black!" you exclaim. "He's just like me."

Kevin from Yale is probably a great guy, but let me ask you something: do you know what Kevin feels like when he walks into a room and realizes that, yet again, he is the only Black person there? When he walks into a meeting and knows that he has to represent every Black male professional out there? Kevin from Yale is everyone's *one* Black friend. Do you understand the mental toll it takes on Kevin from Yale to have been Kevin from Yale every single day of his professional life?

Kevin from Yale wears his pocket-handkerchief just right. Kevin from Yale never says "aks" instead of "ask." Kevin from Yale never loses his temper at work. Kevin from Yale never wears casual jeans on Fridays. Kevin from Yale works late and shows up early the next morning. Kevin from Yale accepts food from the Black server at the antebellum mansion and holds his grimace inside. Kevin from Yale has to listen to grown men call him "My boy!"

Kevin from Yale works hard to make sure no one thinks he is anything *but* Kevin from Yale, because the second he stumbles – the second he mispronounces a word, raises his voice, plays that music, has a scuff on his shoe, or wobbles on the tightrope on which he is walking is the second that someone turns to him and thinks, unconsciously or not, "I guess he's just like the rest of *them*." Then he doesn't get that project because "he's not the right fit." They don't consider him for a promotion because "he's not ready yet." They don't assign him to that client because "he has some rough edges." And because Kevin is carrying an entire race on his back, when he does stumble, he hears the other whisper: "Well, we're never hiring someone like *him* again."

That's how easy it is to be Kevin from Yale.

Your Culture Does Not Include Everyone

Anybody in a marginalized group knows that our ways of speaking, acting, and even thinking are not as valued as those of the majority. So, we try. We try to be someone else every time we walk in your doors. We vet our thoughts, we check our behaviors, we correct our actions, we change our accents, we switch our dialects, over and over again, while conforming to norms and values that won't change for us and were decided when many of us weren't even allowed in the room.

This might look completely effortless to you, but inside, many of us are screaming.

That's why we need to understand that culture matters. A culture is a system of rules that affect how we express our-selves as part of a group, a set of agreed-upon expectations in a social community.[1] Those expectations structure how people in the community act toward one another. Culture tells us what behaviors are expected in our workplace, even if we've never fully explained those behaviors to anyone. Everyone just gets it even if they didn't in fact "agree" to it.

Your organization has a culture. The culture was defined by the people who founded the organization, who run the orga-nization, and who are the majority of leadership in the orga-nization, which means that for many companies in corporate America, that culture is White, straight, cisgender, abled, and male. The belief that that culture is neutral and it welcomes everyone is just as false a belief that a person in America can be colorblind to race. Your organization has values, a history, norms and expectations, and a culture that doesn't include everyone, unless they want to assimilate in order to belong.

Henry Ford and the English School

Have you ever heard of Henry Ford's melting pot ceremo-nies? We always talk about how America is this great melting pot, where many cultures, ethnicities, religions, and identities are mixed together and out emerges this one great American identity. Now we know that's not entirely true – we're really more a mosaic than a melting pot. And yet, for a very long time in this country, and specifically for a very long time in the workplace, we tried to make this melting pot metaphor a reality. A great example of that? The Ford Motor Organization.

Back in 1917, the Ford Motor Organization had huge num-bers of Eastern and Southern European immigrants on its rolls, but turnover was 370%, because so many of these immigrants found it hard to adapt from the agrarian economies of their native lands to the industrial economy of Dearborn, Michigan, and also because many couldn't even understand each other.[2]

Enter Henry Ford's English School, designed not just to teach immigrants about assembly lines and how to speak English, but how to become Americans – or, at least, Henry Ford's very specific vision of American White middle-class culture, values, and norms. The school's graduation ceremony even featured a literal melting pot into which graduates in "native dress" would pile in only to come out as Americans:[3]

> Into the gaping pot they went. Then six instructors
> of the Ford School, with long ladles, started stirring.
> "Stir! Stir!" urged the superintendent of the school.
> The six bent to greater efforts. From the pot fluttered
> a flag, held high, then the first of the finished prod-
> uct of the pot appeared, waving his hat. The crowd
> cheered as he mounted the edge and came down
> the steps on the side. Many others followed him. ...
> In contrast to the shabby rags they wore when they
> were unloaded from the ship, all wore neat suits.
> They were American.

Your Organization Is Not a Melting Pot

Now it's been 100 years since Ford's factory. As far as I know, there are no more melting pot ceremonies in America. And yet, for many Americans inside and outside the workplace, we are still descendants of that assimilation belief, of that melting pot approach. The culture that exists in our workplace. The norms we are expected to adopt. The language we need to use. The emotions we are allowed to show. The personal lives we are allowed to bring into the workplace. When we talk about the hard conversations we need to have to move forward on diversity, the honest conversations, this melting pot is exactly what I'm talking about.

The melting pot of corporate America doesn't include everyone; it never did, nor was it ever intended to. Rather, it is meant to reflect norms and values of White men, who founded, built, and occupy leadership positions throughout it. And like Henry Ford before them, if you want to succeed in that culture, then the melting pot of assimilation is the real way to go.

It's why Kimiko changes her name to Kim. It's why Ibrahim doesn't talk about his religion at work. It's why Malcolm greets his Black colleagues with a wide grin and a dap, but his White colleagues with a firm nod and a handshake. "There's no crying in baseball!" Tom Hanks screams in *A League of Their Own*. Not because people don't cry, of course they do, but because baseball was built by people who don't think crying in public is acceptable (except when you win). So those of us who cry, laugh loudly, speak with passion, build collaborative teams, wear big earrings, and say "aks" instead of "ask" – we become something else. We become experts at hiding ourselves so we can succeed. So much so that when a 22-year-old girl simply asks, "How long will I need to do this?" the only answer I can give her is, "for the rest of your career."

That's why when you see Kevin from Yale, all I see is a Black man who has to work every single day just so he can belong. I am a Black woman living in a White neighborhood where my children attend schools with predominantly White families, and the only time I feel like I can be myself is when I go back to my Black spaces. When I am in the majority again, I can laugh loudly and not have someone be scared of me. I can choose to not smile and not have someone think, "She's so unfriendly." I can take my own children to the park and not have someone call me their nanny.

Because the second we stumble, the second we fall out of line, the second we take off that mask, the second we decide to not code switch, the second we decide to no longer, as

Professor Kenji Yoshino puts it, cover in the workplace[4] is the second we are told, either implicitly or explicitly, unconsciously or not, in statements that are made, actions that are expressed, emails we are not CC'ed on, promotions we are not considered for, invitations we are not extended, raised eyebrows at our clothing choices, and turned backs at the playground that "our culture includes everyone but it does not include you."

Those are the old rules of diversity and inclusion. How long will we live by them?

Notes

1. Building cultural competence : innovative activities and models, Author: Kate Berardo; Darla K Deardorff, Publisher: Sterling, Virginia : Stylus, [2012] ©2012
2. Henry Ford : critical evaluations in business and management. Vol. 2, John Cunningham Wood; Michael C Wood, Routledge, 2003.
3. Sollors W. *Beyond Ethnicity: Consent and Descent in American Culture.* Oxford University Press; 1986.
4. Kenji Yoshino, Covering: The hidden assault on our civil rights, New York: Random House, 2006.

Chapter 8

It's Time to Change the Rules

"How long?"

I am back in your office, and it's not Jasmine asking that question. It's me. I'm asking you.

How long will you only promote the business case for diversity, focusing on numbers alone?

How long will you say that it's OK to be biased because everyone is, and here are a few strategies to make it better?

How long will you say that you don't see race and that the color of someone's skin does not affect whether they succeed in the workplace?

How long will you claim that everyone who starts at an organization has the same chance to succeed?

How long will you pretend that your culture is inclusive of everyone and that everyone feels like they belong here?

Those are your old rules of diversity. How long will you live by them?

Do you remember why you came to me in the first place? Look at your Friday afternoon diversity report again. Look at your C-suite again. Look at your board again. Look at your promotions again. Look at that candidate you just lost. Look at that discrimination suit you just settled. Look at that email chain that's on the front page of *The Wall Street Journal*. Look at it all again. How long will you keep doing this over and over again? How long until you are ready to change?

Because it is time to change. It is time to transform "That's how we've always done it" into "This is how we change it." It is time to *try*. To take a risk. To do something that everyone says is crazy but that you know you have to do because of the thousands of people, every single day, who you know are being left out and behind.

I know you can do it. Because that's exactly what I did.

The day Jasmine asked me, "How long?" I decided I was done telling talented minorities that the only way they could succeed was to be someone else. I was tired of all the books about executive presence and louder voices. I was tired of telling marginalized people that they are the only ones who need to change. It was time to tell the workplace that it needed to change as well. Five months later, I left my full-time job for good and started my new career.

Ever since, I have witnessed firsthand what change can be. I have traveled to cities and companies to bring the truths about why we are stuck on diversity to everyone. People around the world have watched my videos, followed me on social media, listened to me on podcasts, read my articles, and seen my TEDx Talk. They've done more than just listen; they have stood up and cheered. They have hugged me and cried. They have written me letters, Facebook comments, and LinkedIn posts; called me; and seen me on the street and said, "I know you! And you see me!" This has been a movement – one that I am so grateful to see explode.

Now it's your turn. Are you willing to abandon the old rules of diversity? Are you willing to follow the new rules of equity? Because, remember, our goal isn't diversity. Our goal is inclusion. If you are ready, then the next part of this book is for you. But make sure you're ready because this is where the real test begins.

As you embark on this journey, you will hear audacious ideas – revolutionary ideas – and you may think they're ridiculous. They would never work here! But what if "the way things are" didn't have to be "the way things are"? What if you could change them? What if the people who could make that change happen were all sitting there in your organization, but their ideas weren't being heard? What if you listened to them? What if you didn't just make them change the way they worked? What if you changed the way *you* worked instead?

You change the rules, you change the workplace for good – for you, for your coworkers, and for the generations to follow you both.

Let's go.

Chapter 9

New Rule of Equity #1. Make the People Case for Inclusion

Tell Them About the People!

There's a famous story, perhaps apocryphal, about the legend-
ary gospel singer Mahalia Jackson and Dr. Martin Luther King,
Jr. In 1963, Dr. King was set to deliver a speech in front of
thousands at the Washington Monument. In drafting what he
was going to say, he couldn't decide which of two things to
focus on: the metaphor of America having written a bad check
to its Black citizens or a metaphor based on multiracial har-
mony that had come to him in a dream.

The printed version of Dr. King's speech focused on the
metaphor of a bounced check, and even as he began to read
the speech on the day of the March on Washington he was
ready to go in that direction – that is, until gospel singer,
Mahalia Jackson shouted the words that would remake history:
"Martin! Tell them about the dream."

Dr. King looked at the 250,000 people gathered in front of
him, and he told them about his dream.

Can you imagine how different history might have been if the "I Have a Dream" speech had been the "America Has Bounced Her Check" speech? Still true, but much less effective for the goal that Dr. King was trying to achieve: convincing millions of White Americans to end racism in the nation.

As a leader reading this book, I need you to do me a favor. Go out there and talk to your organization about business strategies and the bottom line and why that should matter for diversity and inclusion work. As you do so, think of me as Mahalia Jackson standing next to you urging, "Tell them about the people!"

I want you to tell them about the people. The thousands of men and women who are not thriving in your workplace. Stop telling me that my diversity matters because it makes more money or makes your team stronger. Start telling me that my diversity matters because I matter. Because people matter. Because their stories matter. Because their isolation matters. Because their death by a thousand cuts matters. Because this organization cares about people and it wants people to succeed. That's diversity not centered on money management or financial gain. It's diversity not centered on the latest and greatest branded strategy your consulting firm decides to sell you (hint, that strategy will change in three years). That's *inclusion* centered on people.

People-Centered Inclusion

People-centered inclusion is just that: centering inclusion on people. People are the beating heart that your organization relies on to survive. Their decision to commit to you as a leader, believe in your vision, follow your direction, incorporate your feedback, power your strategies, and help your business grow is only outmatched by your ability to lead them. You have to meet people where they are – to encourage their creativity, to ensure that their creativity results in production, to translate your goals into aspirations they can meet, and to help them reach the heights you know they can achieve.

If you want to truly lead this world of collaborators, innovators, and change makers, let people follow you not because they have to but because they want to. Help them feel liked, cared for, included, valued, and trusted. Help them produce in a world that emphasizes efficiency and shortcuts over long-term thinking. Help develop them, but most of all, *see them.* See them for who they are and what they can achieve.

Because the secret is people. And people want what people have always wanted. They want to rise; they want to succeed; they want to love; they want to worship; they want to be safe; and they want to matter, in their communities, in their cities, in their countries, and in their organizations, with the whole of their being.

Centering inclusion on people means making sure initiatives, strategies, and systems work for them. It means understanding the cultural differences among workers and crafting plans that take those differences into account. It means recognizing the challenges that first-generation professionals have and designing policies to fit them. It means acknowledging the difficulties that your teams across the globe may have being included and working to address them. It means empathizing with the struggle of someone undergoing gender transition – and ensuring that organization benefits reflect that.

An organization that centers its inclusion on people, rather than the business case, isn't one that just understands and values differences; it actually fixes systems to *make those differences work* for the people who work there and the organization they work in.

"Tell them about the people!" Because that's what inclusion is all about.

How do you center inclusion on people? Here is how I want you to start.

Start with Respect

Respect simply means recognizing the equal value of someone else's humanity. What's known as the Platinum Rule – "Treat people the way they want to be treated" – is a good starting point, but I prefer a different rule: "Respect others because of who *you* are, not because of who *they* are." You should have a strong moral compass within you that says every person you encounter deserves respect.

Think about it this way: Someone whose values you don't share, whose perspective you have yet to understand, whose actions you can't empathize with, is falling off a cliff. Do you let them fall because of who they are? Or do you give them a hand and save their life because of who *you* are? That's how vitally important respect is – to your workplace and to our civilization.

Respect requires you to recognize your own faults by acknowledging how actions you took or statements you made hurt someone else. It means being humble enough to admit you were wrong, that what you said or did hurt someone else, and also being courageous enough to make amends. If it means that you need to send out an email telling folks to stop touching people's hair at work, then so be it. Make respect actionable, not just aspirational.

I often hear from clients that they become frustrated when marginalized employees get angry at them for saying or doing the wrong thing. "I didn't know!" they exclaim. We so often ask minorities to take on the role of an educator over and over again. So, let me change the narrative a bit. I want to try another analogy that I heard once. Someone steps on your foot once. That hurts. You ignore it. Then it happens again. And again. And again. And again. Sometimes you ignore it. Sometimes you speak up. Then, finally, the hundredth time someone does it; that's *it* – you get angry. Respect means recognizing that anger is as valid an emotion as any other and then doing the work – to learn, to apologize, to grow – without relying on the person whose foot you just stepped on to tell you why it hurt again.

Listen to Learn

How do we make respect matter? Start with listening. Be open to other perspectives; engage in dialogue, not debate, and always thank someone for listening when your conversation has concluded.

If you are in the majority, remember to listen to learn. Everyone has a story to tell, but for minorities in majority spaces, that story has often been ignored, suppressed, or told by majority voices. Listen to your peers; if and when they share their stories, learn from what they say. Don't gaslight them by denying their lived experiences. If someone tells you, "I don't feel welcome at this organization event," your response shouldn't be, "Well, that's not true at all." Instead, say, "Tell me more. Why do you think that?" – and, more important, "What can we do to change it?"

Listening to learn applies outside of your own personal inclusion journey. In order for inclusion to take root in an organization, we need to encourage a culture of listening. Listening to new ideas. Listening to novel solutions. Listening to feedback from your employees. Listening to critiques of proposed solutions. Listening to team members who do not feel empowered to share and giving them platforms to speak. Listening to their ideas and allowing them to take flight.

Lean into the Discomfort

Let's be real. Listening to these stories is likely to make you feel uncomfortable. You will hear things and feel things that may make you angry. You may enter spaces where you don't know if you are welcome. You may get pushback from people you thought were your friends. You may be asked questions that you don't know the answers to. You may have to speak out when you know the reaction will not be positive.

You know what I have to say to that? Welcome to what it feels like to be a minority in a majority space! Just because many of us have learned how to navigate it, does not mean we don't feel it. Discomfort. Every. Single. Day.

I once had a conversation with a White friend who lamented that she would feel uncomfortable attending an all-Black church. I responded that I understood because I have been in more all-White churches than I can count, and all-White conference rooms, all-White elevators, and all-White schools, bars, weddings, and baseball games. Minorities live and breathe in majority spaces. Try doing the same.

Start entering spaces where you are the minority. Enter them respectfully. Enter to listen and to learn. Visit neighborhoods that are primarily minority. Read books by marginalized authors. Browse websites based on identities other than your own. Continue to take part in new situations where you will feel out of place and learn from your discomfort. Most of all, stay the course even when you misstep. When you get tired of thinking about equity and just want to be comfortable again, think about Kevin from Yale. He does it every day. You can, too.

Commit Yourself Publicly to Inclusion

To be clear, I am not just talking about your organization committing itself to inclusion by sharing its values or drafting a strategic plan (we'll talk about that next). I'm talking about you. People-centered inclusion means you as a leader declaring that you are standing up for people. I want you to explain why inclusion should matter for the organization. I want you to explain what actions are not inclusive and what policies are not equitable. Every single diversity and inclusion practitioner will tell you that their work cannot succeed if leadership is not all the way on board. Publicly acknowledge the inclusion journey that you are on and commit yourself to staying on that course.

Speaking of those diversity and inclusion practitioners, publicly acknowledging your commitment to inclusion means supporting them as well. Whether a full-time executive or a part-time employee, ensure that the people who are in charge of navigating this change have the resources, the buy-in, and the help they need to make that change happen. They need to be influencers. They need people to listen to them. They need you to support them. They need their initiatives to take root. But you know what they *don't* need? Another article on why their jobs are useless. Please stop forwarding those articles to them. They've already read them all. Twice!

Be More Than an Ally – Be an Upstander

Here's the next action I need from you. To borrow a term from the LGBTQ+ community, be an "ally." An ally is any person who supports, empowers, or stands up for another person or a group of people.[1] Someone who does not make the pain of another's their own or centers the conversation on themselves but rather transfers the benefits of their privilege to someone else.[2]

That's what an ally is. But I want more than that from you. I want you to be an ally in the way they were allies fighting wars against countries. They used their resources and their skills and their best people, and they stood up and fought on their ally's behalf. In her 2017 *Time* cover story about Harvey Weinstein, attorney and journalist Jill Fillipovic had this to say about male allies:

> Every woman … knows the pretty good men who
> aren't predators, but who intentionally or tacitly cre-
> ate the conditions for the predation, degradation or
> even just marginalization of women: the men who
> make up all-male boards and executive leadership,
> who don't want to create discomfort by challenging
> sexism from friends or co-workers, who hire and
> mentor and promote younger men who remind them
> of themselves, who go silent on "women's issues."[3]

Allyship isn't silent. Allyship isn't passive. Allyship is *work*,
which is why I want to use another term for an ally that
I think gets to the heart of the work that they need to do.
I don't just want an ally who stands back and watches; I
want an *upstander* who changes the world. Coined by dip-
lomat Samantha Powers, the term "upstander" refers to "[a]
person who speaks or acts in support of an individual or
cause."[4] That's what I want you to become. When you see
something problematic, don't ignore it, stand up, and speak
out about it.

An upstander reinforces that certain behaviors are not
allowed here. An upstander instills community norms that
everyone can abide by. An upstander lets marginalized
employees know that they have a champion and an advocate
willing to create a safe community for them, where targeting,
discrimination, racism, and harassment are not tolerated. An
upstander puts people in their own community on notice that
they should stand up against this behavior as well.

Be an upstander. Speak up when someone repeats what
a woman already said in a meeting. Speak up when someone sends a joke mocking the new transgender hire. Speak
up when someone dismisses someone else struggling with
depression. Because many of those people aren't in the rooms
where those statements are being made. They're not on the
email chains where those memes are being forwarded. If you
are, be an upstander. Stand up to injustice.

Allyship Is Not Enough; Be an Antiracist

Which means allyship is only the start. I want those of you who are in White-majority organizations, living in a White-majority nation, run by White-majority leadership, with our nation's long history of racism, to be more than an ally. I want you to be an antiracist.

Antiracist means that when there are policies that promote racial inequality, you work to change them. As Dr. Ibram X. Kendi explains in his book, *How to be An Antiracist*, an antiracist is "one who is expressing the idea that racial groups are equals and none needs developing, and is supporting policy that reduces racial inequality."[5] As an antiracist leader, you consistently work at identifying racism in every system, in every structure, in every policy and practice in your organization, and ensure that power is redistributed equally and equitably.[6]

Does that seem like a lot of work? It absolutely is. But does that mean you can't start? It does not. And I know you can. Because no one is born into this country an antiracist, not in a country with its history books, its literary canon, its music and movies, its government leaders, its justice system, its laws and legislation, and its majority culture, rooted in White supremacy. Instead, you are raised to be an antiracist. You are taught to be an antiracist. You learn to be antiracist. You learn that it is not enough to say someone should do something about it. You learn to say I will do something about it.

So, you learn to be an antiracist when a 12-year-old Black boy named Tamir Rice gets shot and killed. When a Black woman named Sandra Bland is arrested for not using her turn signal and is found hanged in her jail cell. When a Black man named Dontre Hamilton gets shot 14 times. When a Black man named Eric Garner gets choked to death. When a Black boy named Laquan McDonald is walking away from police officers and is shot 16 times. And when a 17-year-old boy is heading home after buying a pack of Skittles and a man stalks and kills him. You learn to be an antiracist as you listen over the next year politicians and pundits and lawyers and eventually a jury, devalue Trayvon Martin's life to the point where a large percentage of the country firmly believed that it was a 17-year-old boy's fault that a stranger had shot him to death. You learn when and when and when and when.

You learn to be an antiracist when you listen to the justifications, the devil's advocates, the "Well, actually." "Well, actually, he was doing something wrong." He was holding a BB gun. He was holding a knife. She was sleeping on a bench. He was fighting back. She said no to the police officer. "It wasn't about race!" they say. They did this so they deserved that. Is that your policing? Is that your justice system? And is that what living while Black means, that I must be perfect so I can stay alive?

If it does, then let's talk about being perfect. Let's talk about Black people sitting in a coffee shop, or shopping at a makeup store, or boarding an airplane, or talking on a phone, or babysitting a child, or selling water on the street, and told in no uncertain terms that they are interlopers there. Let me tell you about the many Black men and women stopped, interrogated, and arrested by police officers for no other reason than because they are Black.

And now I am a Black employee. I come into your workplace. Here's what I will tell you. I will tell you that the injustices do not end at that office door. They endure in the death by a thousand cuts. They endure in being passed over, looked over, isolated, alone, ignored. When I know that the white leaders won't stop by my office to chat, that we won't talk about shared schools and neighborhoods and friends, that I won't get roped into a last minute deal, that I won't get spoken about in rooms as the next rising star, when my culture and my life experiences aren't reflected at work, when people call me the diversity hire, when my presence as a Black person makes them uncomfortable because they don't know my "culture", that as much as I try to do everything right, to assimilate, to fit in, cut by cut by cut, when I leave, as almost all of us do, I am told I didn't want it enough to stay.

No one is born into this country an antiracist. You learn to be an antiracist when you learn the history of racism in America, when you see the reality of racism in America, when you live the reality of racism in America. You learn to be an antiracist because you live in a country where you can no longer look away from the inequity created and amplified by racism, where you begin to understand how you as an individual have contributed to that inequity, and where you commit yourself to the work of change.

Are you uncomfortable again? Because here's the truth about change. It doesn't happen from a space of comfort. Transforming systems of inequity, inside and outside the workplace, will not happen if people stay comfortable with them. It's hard, uncomfortable, and part of the work of change.

Be an antiracist in your life and your work. Be an antiracist in your neighborhood, your children's school, your volunteer boards, and your own organization. While you do that, remember this. Being an antiracist is not easy. Highlighting behavior that many in the majority have been comfortable for years letting slide, so comfortable that it has become normalized, is not likely to make you the most popular person in the C-suite. You will feel uncomfortable. You could be attacked. You might lose friends. That's why I don't start the new rules with the business case. The business case doesn't make you commit to the work. The business case doesn't make you change an unequal playing field. The business case doesn't make you keep going when everyone else says you should stop. That's why I start with the people. "Tell them about the people!" Remember the people. Fight for the people.

Notes

1. https://ctb.ku.edu/en/table-of-contents/culture/cultural-competence/be-an-ally/main
2. www.guidetoallyship.com/
3. https://time.com/4979258/harvey-weinstein-what-happens-next/?utm_campaign=time&utm_source=twitter.com&utm_medium=social&xid=time_socialflow_twitter
4. www.facinghistory.org/upstander
5. How to Be an Antiracist. New York: One World. Kendi, Ibram X., How to Be an Antiracist. New York: One World, 2019.
6. http://www.aclrc.com/antiracism-defined

Chapter 10

New Rule of Equity #2. Build a Data-Driven Equity Strategy

The thing about the check though is that it is a powerful motivator for a lot of people. Dr. King wouldn't have used that metaphor if it weren't. You tell someone the image of a bad check being cashed, and they nod because they understand money.

Money, money, money.
Money, money.
Money.

So back to you, people-centered leader. I'm glad you're on board. Now let's talk the business case. The real business case. Don't end with explaining broadly why you're losing money, employees, recruits or missing out on markets. Go beyond that. Connect equity directly to the business strategy of *your* organization. Equity will not matter until you make it a core goal of your business.

Many organizations have spent millions of dollars trying to do this, only to make little to no progress elevating marginalized employees to the C-suite. If you are still trying to commodify your minority employees, if you are still trying to shrug off bias, if you still argue you don't "see race," if you still think everyone starts at the same starting line, and if you still think your culture already includes everyone – if you still believe all of that, then no number of highly paid experts can possibly create a strategy for you that will be successful.

You want to know why diversity and equity leaders have such high turnover rates? Because companies spend so much time on strategy and so little time on the hard work of change. And so these extremely experienced, practical, and highly talented leaders recognize very quickly that all the strategies in the world will make no difference if companies are unwilling to change.

People are not widgets. Identities are not commodities. Inclusion is not a line item in your financial report. So yes, do the hard work of explaining why recruiting, retaining, and leading a diverse workforce is important but also understand that if profit is your motivation for supporting equity, then you aren't going to have marginalized folks on board for long for all the real, deep, painful change that needs to happen for successful initiatives to take root. Instead, I suggest you follow the five steps below for designing a strategic equity plan.

Step 1: Assemble Your Equity Avengers and Craft a Mission Statement

First, you need to know who you have on your team. You may have a full-time diversity professional, or you may not, but either way, a diversity professional alone cannot do the work that organization leadership is supposed to do. It's time to assemble your strike team, your task force, your planning committee, your squad, your Super Friends, your Seal Team 6, your Avengers – the group of employees who will oversee your equity strategy. Ensure board members or management committee members are part of your team.

Once your team is assembled, craft your mission statement. Start by having a launch meeting where each person on the team discusses what equity means to them, to the organization, and to clients. Discuss what goals you have for the organization. Do you want to reach new global markets? New domestic markets? More access to new clients or government contracts? What does equity mean for your value proposition, for your market share, for recruiting?

After you've put together your business case, create a vision statement. Based on the information that you have gathered, what is your organization's vision for equity? What is the goal? I also want you to make a values statement. Look at the values you have publicly listed as an organization – say, innovation, excellence, or integrity – and tie in your vision for equity to those values. Why does equity drive innovation? Why is equity an excellence metric? How does equity impact our integrity?

Next, you'll connect the vision and values statements to draft a mission statement – not for the organization but for your team. Members of the team need to know why they are taking time out of their very busy days to do this. They want to feel motivated and inspired. So, let's motivate them with a mission statement. Here's a simple example:

The mission of the Avengers Strike Force Squad on Inclusion is to design a people-centered space at Devlin where differences are encouraged, identities are respected, and individuals are allowed an equal chance to succeed.

If you want to tie in how equity benefits the organization, you can do that in your mission statement, too: "Because we at Devlin recognize that innovation and customer success rely on everyone in this organization belonging and succeeding here."

Step 2: Propose Preliminary Goals for Equity

Now it's time to draft the preliminary equity goals that your organization hopes to achieve. You will revise these later, but right now you should establish some key objectives. Possible examples might be to place minority employees in supervisory roles, increase minority recruitment and retention rates, create structured succession plans, diversify outside vendors, or reduce the number of discrimination and harassment complaints received by HR. Those are all achievable goals. However, they need to be refined. It's time to dig deep.

Step 3: Do a Dig Deep Data Dive to Understand Where You Are Falling Short

This step is the heart and soul of change. So many companies are either in compliance mode ("as long as certain boxes are checked, we're OK") or in programming mode ("let's throw a bunch of initiatives at the wall and see what sticks") when it comes to equity when they should really be in dig deep data mode ("what does the objective reality on the ground tell us?"). For example, it's very easy to overestimate how many people with disabilities you have in leadership roles or how many Latinx hires you fail to promote until you dive into the cold, hard facts.

Now, I'll be honest. This is a lot of work, and it does require some training in data analysis. You may want to hire a consultant to do this work. But if you don't, you know who should have the knowledge and training to do this work? Your talent management team. Human resources. People. They are right there, in your companies, right now, with access to all of this data. They are overseeing performance evaluations. They are running mentoring programs. They are doing the diversity surveys. They are collecting the demographic data. They are conducting exit interviews. Some companies have dozens of people on their human resources team. Some only have one. Utilize their expertise. Utilize their skill sets. No, equity should not be sandwiched away into human resources. But instead of relying on your squad to do the work of data analysis, lean on your HR team to do the same.

Here are some specific areas to explore when conducting this deep dive:

Organizational structure. List every department in the organization in every branch and office. For each department,
list any positions held by minority employees and their
levels (e.g., entry-level, mid-level, executive). Next, list the
number of minority employees organization wide and
determine the following: attrition rates, promotion rates,
salary ranges, and bonus ranges. Finally, compare organization demographic data to other publicly available data.

Project assignments. Next up is the work. It is a truth uni-
versally acknowledged that all work is not created equal
and who gets the "quality" work is a huge determining
factor in who succeeds and who does not. Remember
Dave and Jasmine? Dive into the work. Collaborate with
team leads and department heads to determine which
assignments are more or less challenging or high-profile
and then ask them how these teams are formed. Who
chooses the members? What are the criteria for inclusion?
Is there any oversight of how work is assigned? How is
labor divided among demographic groups within teams?
If you don't have a team-based system or have a very
small organization, ask similar questions: What are the
criteria for success? Are our minority employees on that
track to success?

Culture, perks, and benefits. Next up, it's time to review
your culture and your benefits. Start with culture. Review
office activities and office perks to determine whether
they benefit one group over another, or are more appeal-
ing to certain demographics than others. So many

startups I consult with have ping pong out and free beer in the kitchen. What type of socializing does that prioritize? What messaging are you sending about the type of people you think are welcome there?

Culture is only one part of it. Review your policies too, particularly the ones that promote work–life balance. Review parental leave, caregiver leave, backup childcare, flex work, sabbaticals, and promotion tracks. Who is taking advantage of these? Are they available to everyone in the office? For leave, in particular, what are you seeing when employees return from leave? Who stays and who goes? Does the work change? Do the evaluations change? Also, are there perks that are available only to some of your employees and not to others? Not based on tenure, but based on status. If so, then consider what message that is sending about who you think is valuable to the organization.

Mentoring relationships and succession planning. I'm not going to spend too much time on mentoring because corporate America has been mentoring marginalized professionals since Day 1 and, well, you've seen the numbers. But it *is* important to figure out who is being mentored (formally or informally) and who isn't, in case certain people are inheriting more valuable clients than others. If marginalized employees aren't even under consideration to inherit a client or business line, then of course they won't rise to the C-suite. For this reason, having an effective succession management system in place with checks and balances to ensure that system doesn't fall prey to bias is crucial to meet pipeline challenges.

Take a look at who has inherited clients, customers, and long-term work. How did they inherit them? Who did they meet? What criteria did they have to satisfy? Was inheriting clients open to anyone else? Was there any type of oversight from the organization? So many marginalized professionals stall on the ladder of success because they don't have the client or customer base needed to get serious consideration for the higher-level organization positions. But if they never had access to them, how could they have obtained them? It's a Catch-22 that your team needs to understand in order to address.

Performance evaluations. Pick a business unit, a demographic category, and a group of people to focus on (people who have left a business unit, for example, or who we have been identified as star performers). Review their evaluations to find patterns in word choice, intensity, delivery, and response. Examine the words used and the ratings assigned. Can you discern patterns of where people got off track or succeeded? What are the scoring trends for minority groups (if any)? Is there a particularly problematic sector, manager, or team approach? Look for trends in the data, because those trends will tell you where the barriers lie.

Recruitment and onboarding. Take your job postings for the last 20 open positions at your organization and review the following:

Where you posted them

Click and application rates

Where recruiting teams were sent and which schools and organizations they worked with

What inquiries or hires came from those schools and organizations

What resumes were looked at; interviews scheduled; offers made, accepted, and declined

Any hiring tests given and how these were evaluated

Any non-test skills evaluated (e.g., personality, cultural fit) and by whom

Exit interviews for those who have left any of the positions

As much as you can, break this all down by demographic. Once you do all of that, you'll have a very good sense of your recruiting picture. Who is coming in, where are they going, who is being left behind, and any evidence that you might need of bias.

Professional development. Review any training programs related to leadership, mentoring, and management. Who is utilizing those programs? What's their feedback? If you have minority employees go through an executive coaching or leadership development program, how does that process affect retention and long-term success?

Climate analysis. Now that you've obtained all this data using information readily available to you, do a climate analysis. You can do a simple survey, you can have focus groups, you can have anonymous questionnaires. Whatever approach you use, you want to find the answers to the following questions:

Do your employees *with marginalized identities* feel like they are able to succeed here?

Are they satisfied with their work?

Do they feel like they have the resources they need to get ahead?

Do they believe in the values of the organization?

Do they feel included in the organization?

Use the answers you receive to establish a good sense of how your organization feels to the marginalized employees who you are trying to retain.

Step 4: Design SMART Goals Based on the Data

Now it is time to change the rules. Let's fix the systems of inequity. Our focus is fixing broken systems, not simply making folks aware they exist.

After completing the Dig Deep Data Dive, work with your team to re-develop each of your equity goals, keeping in mind the information uncovered during your dig deep data dive. I make fun of "management consultant-speak," but I do agree that goals should be:

Specific
Measurable
Attainable
Realistic
Timebound

For each group or department, list your SMART goals as they relate to equity and explain in detail how each group or department will achieve each goal. Set out a timeline, due dates, evaluation plan, and reporting format. Develop a system for groups or departments to compare progress and share ideas and solutions. Then, connect these goals to the organization's business drivers. Give me a value proposition for equity. How would you convince your most jaded shareholders that your goals matter? Because none of this work will matter at all if the decision makers at your organization aren't committed to seeing it through.

Step 5: Hold Managers Accountable for Achieving Those Goals

You have your mission statement. You have your data. You have your SMART goals. Maybe you even combined them all into a 40-page strategic plan. But now comes the hard part. Holding managers accountable for meeting, or failing to meet, those goals.

For example, let's say you have a goal of increasing the percentage of Latinx managers at your organization. That's a big goal that you'll probably break down into various tasks: delivering quality assignments to Latinx employees, introducing them to clients, engaging coaches, improving evaluation metrics, and increasing their organizational visibility. Who is accountable for each step? And please don't make it someone in HR or the organization's diversity practitioner. The person accountable should be intimately involved with the work at hand.

Next you must establish *how* to hold managers accountable for meeting goals. Accountability means more than casual check-ins to make sure everything is going well; it usually requires a combination of carrots and sticks. I would love to live in a world where people are committed to equity simply because it's the right thing to do, but instead we live in a world beholden to profit margins. So make that world work for you. Determine incentives for success and penalties for failure. Incorporate equity goals into your manager's objectives and have mandatory meetings with management on the status of equity goals.

Most important of all, though, is to tie meeting those equity goals to compensation. Your marginalized protégé gets promoted? You get a bonus! You recommend a marginalized hire who meets success criteria? You get a bonus! Your marginalized direct reports all increased their evaluation scores across the board? Everyone gets a bonus! All those dinners and recruiting and interviews – that I'd like to point out your minority employees have been doing for free for years – you get a bonus, and you get a bonus, and you get a bonus. Use the power of your piggy bank. Because in my ideal world, I would like diversity to matter without having to put money behind it. In the real world, I know it won't. Not yet.

Congratulations, You Have a Strategic Plan!

Now you have your plan, but you still need buy-in from your organization. You as a leader need to give them a compelling reason for focusing on equity. You need to explain the rationale for why you are doing this. Are you ready to show the data? Are you ready to share your goals? Are you ready to assign employees to task forces to meet those goals? Are you ready to center your work on the experiences and isolation of your minority employees rather than the comfort and convenience of your majority ones? Too many of the strategic plans

I see are so focused on not making anyone uncomfortable that they do little to move the equity needle. If the reason to be so meek in your strategic plan is because you are concerned that your employees will protest and leave, then you are starting from the wrong place. You need your employees to buy into equity, not into a strategic plan. It's once they've bought in that the hard work of change really begins.

How can you do that? Remember, the Dig Deep Data Dive. Here's the other reason I made you do that – because data is your ally.

In 2018, Meghan Markle married Prince Harry of the United Kingdom. Over the next two years, she was subject to the most racist news stories about everything from her personality to her charity work to her wedding dress to her food choices to her skills as a mother. Then Buzzfeed published an article showing, in detail by exacting detail, how slanted the coverage of Meghan was compared to that of her sister-in-law, Kate.[1] Kate used lilies of the valley for her wedding bouquet? Joyous. Meghan used lilies of the valley for hers? Poisonous to children! Kate loves avocado? How sweet. Meghan loves avocado? Human rights abuse!

For some, it was vindication for what they had long believed, that Meghan really was getting raked across the coals for the simple crime of being Black. For others, it was a realization that while they had tried to allay the negative media coverage into, "Well, actually, all royal families get this," they had not reckoned with the anti-Blackness that colored every headline. That is, until they were shown the evidence.

Show the data. Show the statistics. Show the receipts. Show the narrowing path to the C-suite for everyone except White men in your organization. The data is what shocks people. The data is what makes them listen. The data is always the best clapback in the world. Some will still argue, but many more will be ready to sit down and do the hard work of change.

Note

1. www.buzzfeednews.com/article/ellievhall/meghan-markle-kate-middleton-double-standards-royal

Chapter 11

New Rule of Equity #3. Want to Hire the "Right Fit"? Use Competencies to Find Them

If there were a diversity and inclusion fairy godmother, the one wish I would ask of them is to eliminate the phrase the "right fit" forever. We *have* to stop hiring, staffing, and promoting people just because we believe they are the "right fit." The "right fit" feeds straight into our biases and expectations of people and won't get us the benefits of diversity. A "right fit" mentality means hiring or promoting someone who you think "checks all the boxes" without recognizing that they don't have the right skills for the role. Stop focusing on the right fit. Start focusing on competencies instead.

Answer me this: What does it take to *really* succeed in your organization? A lot of companies have competencies, but the truth is many of them have been designed by, and are designed with, the majority in mind. I want you to go find out not what makes the majority succeed but what makes the minority *not* succeed. I want you to answer the essential question, "At what point do minority employee and majority employee achievements diverge?" What does it actually take to get someone from one level of your organization to the next? Is it obvious, or is there a secret path that only the in-group knows about? Focus on competencies when you're onboarding, when you're evaluating, when you're promoting, and especially when you're hiring.

Why Competencies Matter for Hiring

Let's talk hiring. Start with step 1: recruiting. If you've done the work and designed your competencies to allow for the success of your minority employees, then you are going to do a much better job of recruiting the type of people who will actually succeed in your firm rather than just make good drinking buddies.

Start by reviewing the language of your job postings. Are you using words that appeal more to men than to women, or that might turn off people from other identity groups? Are you using phrases like "good fit" that suggest a work culture not inclusive of difference? Are you using problematic language to describe your organization's demographics? Crucially, are you sharing your organization's commitment to equity in every job posting? Addressing all these questions will go a long way toward ensuring a workforce that is both competent and inclusive of difference.

Remember: Unicorns Don't Exist

Every organization is looking for the unicorn – that one person who checks all the right boxes. The unicorn went to the right school, has all the right experience, and worked with the right people. The unicorn meets all our qualifications and needs no additional training. The unicorn also thinks our

jokes are funny, dresses like us, and lives in our neighborhoods. The unicorn is just right, just perfect – and a minority
hire, too! Thank goodness for that.

There's only one problem. Come here. Are you listening
closely?
UNICORNS! DO! NOT! EXIST!

A unicorn is a fictional creature. It does not exist in real life,
and it certainly does not exist in your workplace. Thousands
upon thousands of highly qualified minority folks apply for
jobs every year, and yet, shockingly, companies simply cannot
find any that are highly qualified. Let me humbly propose an
alternate narrative: The problem isn't them – it's you. Because
you won't countenance additional training time, or an unfa-
miliar background, or a point of view informed by a different
lived reality.

Plus, there's this truth. We say we're looking for unicorns,
but we're often only looking for unicorns when that person
is a minority. Because if they're not a unicorn, you need to
justify over and over again why you hired them. It's why Black
Thomas Meyer's memo gets corrected at such a higher rate
than White Thomas Meyer's. We didn't lower our standards
for the White Thomas Meyer; we just raised our standards for
the Black one. So let's give the minority hire additional hoops
to jump through. Let's give the minority hire the expectations
of failure rather than success. Let's set the minority hire without the social network they need to succeed. Let's judge the
minority hire's answers on a different level. Let's make them
work harder just so they can get a foot in the door, and when
they don't succeed, let's congratulate ourselves for not "low-
ering our standards." But make sure to sign that multi-year
contract with the coaching company for the White manager so
he can improve how he "works with people."

Forget unicorns. Hire for skill sets. Hire for knowledge.
Hire for potential. Don't hire someone just because they're the

right fit – and don't reject them just because your biases tell you they aren't.

But There's No One to Recruit!

It astonishes me how many organizations believe they can simply put up a listing on the Internet and watch minority candidates flock to it. Up to 85% of all jobs are filled by networking, which means people apply for jobs that their friends tell them about.[1] And when the average White American has 91 White friends and 9 friends of color? That means your search is already hampered before it starts.

So what's the solution? Go out and find diverse candidates! Send recruiters to minority–majority campuses and minority events. And don't just send people from HR – send people who do the work that you want to hire for. Have them meet the heads of affinity groups at universities. Invite minority candidates to visit your office. Host events for them in your building or online. Assign employees to follow up with them individually to answer any questions they may have.

That's just for entry-level positions. If you're hiring at the managerial or executive level, you may want to use a recruiting organization. If you do, be sure to specifically ask that the organization send you a diverse slate of candidates. Even better, work with a recruiting organization that specializes in diverse hires.

It also helps to do research of your own and incentivize people away from their current employers. Encourage your employees to report back any minority speakers who impress them at conferences or competitors whose work they admire. Find out their names. Get introduced to them. And when the opportunity arises, ask them whether they would be interested in seeing what you have to offer. Try not to make the experience purely transactional. Create a relationship with this person because it's not just about them – it's about their network as well. That person could very well be a super-connector.

A super-connector is someone with a strong and diverse network of potential job candidates. If they share a posting, their pool of acquaintances will see it. If you ask them, they will have some ideas about who might be interested. If you don't have any super-connectors at your workplace, use your own networks to find them. Tell them the story of your organization. Tell them about your commitment to equity.

Of course, in the best-possible scenario, the biggest source of referrals would be a minority executive at your organization who is living proof of your commitment to equity. Nothing, absolutely nothing, can top the example that sets.

That also means this: your employees are going to be your best source for locating minority candidates. Make it known to employees that you are seeking minority candidates. Provide them with incentives to go out to recruiting events and minority job fairs. Equip them with the language to use when they are asked about your organization's equity initiatives. Ensure they fully understand the added value equity brings to the organization as well as the crucial role they play in making inclusion a reality. If you still have a solid relationship with ex-employees from marginalized communities, reach out to them for recommendations.

Revisit Your Assumptions about Who Can Succeed

Lost that candidate, did you? Because there's only a handful of minority candidates at the level that you want to recruit at. Assuming you've checked your biases, you've designed competencies, and you still can't find anyone suited for the job. I'd suggest two things.

First, consider potential hires who don't have the "right degree" or the "right experience" but who can be trained to fit the role. We don't all come into our workplaces, knowing what we want to be when we grow up. I'm 37, and I'm still finding it out. Why do we create companies assuming that a 22-year-old knows exactly where they should be?

I started out in law in the same place many Black millennials do, in the only fields we know – litigation and transactional work. It took me years to realize how vast and complex the legal profession is. But for a 25-year-old whose parents may not have gone to law school, much less college? Whose first interaction with a law firm might be in her interview? When she's asked what she wants to practice, and her first answer is what she knows from television and her first-year classes. Litigation. That's not good enough. Not if we want to retain the best talent and ensure their success in our organizations.

Be the leader who looks at a marginalized employee's skill set and works with them to identify where in the organization their talents can be put to their best use. Maybe it's where they already are. Maybe it's somewhere else. It's far better to figure that out than to, well, call me in at 9 a.m. on Monday because another minority employee just walked out the door. If nothing else, at least hire a coach for them too.

Second, I would like to humbly suggest that the pipeline is still strong and pumping in your own organization. Use your entry-level candidates and turn them into high-potential candidates. You likely have a far larger diverse talent pool at the entry level of your organization. Focus on retaining them. Focus on advancing them. Focus on ensuring that they have the tools to succeed and eliminating the barriers that prevent their success. You really want your next unicorn? They might be sitting right there in your organization, but you are so focused on recruiting rather than retention that you forgot to grow them.

Use Objective Measures to Score Candidates

Let's say you've done the legwork and gotten some minority candidates. By what criteria are you judging them during interviews? What qualities are you looking for in candidates that would allow them to meet the competencies you've developed? You don't want your interviewers to ask the same questions again and again, so a good way to acquire this information is through a well-designed grading rubric. *Success metric:* entrepreneurship. *Factor:* proactively seeks out new partnership opportunities. *Question for candidate:* tell me about a time where you had to convince a professor or supervisor that your approach was the best one. If you're using a scale of 1–5, what's a 5 answer? What's a 3 answer? What's a 1 answer? Provide your interviewers with questions they can choose from and sample answers that they can correctly score with.

If you really want to cover your bases, give a score to *everything*. If subjective criteria like likability and compatibility are important to you, then develop a rubric for measuring them in a way that takes competencies into account – and, crucially, in a way that can be defended later. It is likely that there will be unexamined biases among your interviewers or the folks in charge of hiring, and rubrics are a great way to keep track of and address these. If one person's score seems at odds with those of others at the organization, don't let that just sit there; ask them to back up their score with evidence. Not with "gut feelings" or "just a sense." "Why do you think that? When did you make that assumption? How did their interview demonstrate that? What about their resume shows that?" This is how you as a leader need to push forward to ensure biases get interrupted from the start. That's why competencies – and all the objectivity that we can create – matter for equity in the workplace.

Use Competencies for Staffing, Evaluations, and Promotions

Finally, I focused on competencies and objectivity for recruiting and hiring, but it doesn't end there. *Use competencies for everything*. For staffing (what are the three skills I need for this project?), for evaluations (what criteria need to be met and what evidence can I demonstrate to support it?), and for promotions (what behaviors demonstrated that they could not meet this requirement?).

Listen, human beings are subjective, but we also aren't robots. You are still going to make subjective decisions. But if bias is System 1 thinking, then these competencies are System 2 thinking. Go back to the Avengers. System 1 is the Hulk going faster, louder, stronger, and angrier. System 2 is Bruce Banner, trying to calm it down, to think, to process, and to slow it down. It's easy to break free and be the Hulk (just ask my five-year-old); it's a lot harder to be Bruce Banner.

Yes, in my dream world, we would get rid of "right fit." But in the real world, I know that people want to be around people that they like. That's why we put competencies in place, to push back against that easy, System 1, Hulk-type, default thinking, and make us reckon with what the "right fit" really means. And if you don't think Jasmine's the right fit, using all the competencies and scores that you have, then be prepared to explain why that is and what that means for her, for you, and the organization that wants an even and equitable playing field for everyone.

Note

1. www.linkedin.com/pulse/new-survey-reveals-85-all-jobs-filled-via-networking-lou-adler/

Chapter 12

New Rule of Equity #4. Build a Community That Works for Your Marginalized Employees

Once you have minority hires onboard, you need to build a community that works for them. Don't just put on your equity lens; put on your cultural competency ones as well. Consider what it might be like for employees from cultures that place a high value on community to work in spaces where they don't see that community around them or that prioritize individualism over collaboration.

I need you to help your marginalized employees find their community in your organization. Many of us work alone despite our many emails and phone calls and regardless of how many coworkers we have. Michelle Obama talks about this challenge in her memoir *Becoming*: not having *our* people to listen to our ideas, to help us with our decisions, to shoot the breeze with us, to congratulate us, to pull us out of a rut when things go wrong. What we have instead is solitude, so thick and so strong that it might as well be a fortress. That's how professional isolation feels.

Please make sure that people within the organization understand the importance of reaching out and connecting. If you need to, create structured avenues for new marginalized hires to socialize with one another. Because community is both a cushion and a trampoline: It embraces you when you fall, but it also bounces you right back up to try again.

Your employees – all of them – need to do the hard work of making community matter. Yes, you might need a workplace Bumble now. I've seen companies do it differently. Managers might ask these new employees out to coffee, for example, take them on a client pitch, or sit in with them on a sales call. Figure out what your marginalized employee would like to do to socialize. Let them suggest a restaurant or an event or a meet-up. It's a good idea to let the new hire suggest where and when in these situations, both so that they feel a sense of buy-in and as a way of showing that you respect their input.

Build Successful Employee Resource Groups

Building a community is everyone's job. So is this one. Creating employee resource groups (ERGs) that work.

I have a love–hate relationship with ERGs. They are the buzziest diversity initiative. However, while everyone may be talking about ERGS, not many understand the true purpose of ERGS, or how to utilize them to advance real change within an organization. Let's make sure you as a leader do.

Let's start by defining what ERGs are, or at least what they are meant to be. Employee resource groups, sometimes referred to as affinity groups, are employee-led groups based on a shared identity of the members of the group, such as race, gender, religion, or any of the dimensions of diversity.[1] While ERGs may seem like they are the newest shiny toy in the equity playbox, ERGs have actually been around since the 1960s as networking organizations for women and people of color.[2] ERGs, ideally, allow employees to feel a sense of belonging and create relationships with those who share their similar backgrounds.[3] Through creating that foundation, those who are members of ERGs can obtain support, understanding, information, and resource sharing that can help ensure their success.

That said, ERGs do a lot more than just produce a community for marginalized employees. They can provide training, idea exchange, client development, executive coaching, and advocacy on behalf of the minority group to leadership.[4] That's why ERGs have evolved from affinity groups to business resource groups to, now, employee resource groups. The name change is supposed to highlight their crucial support for the business drivers of the organization, including a push for more diversity.[5] In one study that surveyed women who had access to a women's networking group, respondents said that their ERGs helped to enhance parental leave benefits, push for more flexibility or better vacation policies, and implement a mentorship or sponsorship program to make it easier to find mentors at work.[6]

When ERGs Don't Work

All that sounds great, right? Well, while ERGs have the potential for huge impact within organizations, they are vulnerable to many pitfalls and can end up being afflicted by various shortcomings. Some even think ERGs are outdated and have been eclipsed by other committees formed within organizations to tackle various equity issues. Companies such as Deloitte have moved beyond ERGs and have created Inclusion Councils that reflect a diverse group of people with different experiences, talents, and perspectives.[7] As one expert stated,

Many [ERGs] were founded with the admirable intention of giving employees who represent a protected class under the law a "safe" place to air ideas, issues or concerns. Some had very prescriptive work baked into their charters, while others were less specific in their objectives. Soon enough, however, objections cropped up. Resource groups for women and minorities were challenged by white men who felt excluded, for example. This type of dissension led employers to try to sharpen their groups' missions or purposes. The real problem, however, is that ERGs seem like relics of a bygone era. Organizations large and small, public and private, are reshaping these groups into diverse teams that are far more strategic and inclusive. One need only look at the proliferation of diversity, equity and inclusion committees to see how much of the work that ERGs used to do has broadened in both scope and depth.[8]

I get the hate against ERGs, I really do. But I go back to that community. For many marginalized employees, having that community is so crucial to making sure they feel like they belong there. I cannot overestimate the power of walking out of a majority workplace and into a room where all the people look exactly like you. That mask that Kevin wears? He can take it off there. That exclusion that Kim feels? She knows the others feel it there too. That bias that Ibrahim is experiencing? That room won't gaslight him into believing it's not true. I have been to so many ERG events where either the entire room is filled with employees of a single-minority identity or that minority group is hosting an event for the whole organization and showcasing the glory of their identity. It is a thing of beauty to watch. I don't want to see that disappear.

Where do ERGs fall short, however? When they don't have honest dialogue. When they don't accomplish anything meaningful in the organization. When they don't add value to the members. When management outsources management work and conflict resolution to an ERG. When the ERGs promote their members' interests but those perspectives are ignored or papered over. When it's just a social network.

Plus, ERGs fail when companies don't understand intersectionality. I consulted for an organization that scheduled their women's ERG meeting at the same time they scheduled their Latinx ERG meeting. If you were a Latina woman, where would you go? And I don't mean to pile on women ERGs, but it is often the case that women ERGs are often White women ERGs and discuss issues of concern that are primarily applicable to White women. If I, as a White woman, am trying to understand how to lean in, I, as a Black woman, would like to say my problem isn't leaning in. My problem is I am seen as too aggressive, too loud, and still not competent enough. My problem isn't just sexism. It's sexism and racism. How are you as a White woman going to help me with that?

How Do We Fix ERGs?

The best way to fix ERGs is to address the shortcomings and needs of the organization before forming your ERG. If you would like to start an ERG, ask yourself these questions: "Which diverse groups are represented or underrepresented in the organization? Is your organization having trouble recruiting women? Are there retention issues with millennial employees? Are you looking to attract Black and Latinx employees?"[9] Addressing these questions during an open and honest assessment of the organization will help ensure that any ERGs that are created are focused on the groups and issues of predominant concern to the organization. Then use your answers to create clear goals and objectives. Why are you creating this ERG? What is the goal that you are trying to achieve? How will this ERG help you meet that goal?

Goals are crucial both at the start and throughout. As you plan your ERG meetings, ensure you articulate a plan for meeting each goal. That will not only help you come up with a budget to propose to leadership; it will also help you with an actionable guide for the fiscal year. However, it is important to note that the most successful ERGs have realistic expectations.[10] So while you should aim high with respect to what your ERG wants to achieve, make sure that those goals are within the ERGs power to achieve.

Because the most important factor for an ERG's success is whether it benefits the organization. To many employees, if the ERG does not have genuine buy-in from the organization's leadership and the power to truly change organizational culture and policies, it will feel like more work. That's why leadership commitment matters. Individual contributors cannot be the only ones committed to the goals of the ERG. It's essential to have an executive be the point person and accountability partner for the ERG. Executive leaders need to champion matters that the ERG brings to their attention to leadership, need to provide the financial contribution to ensure the ERG is able to carry out their activities, and need to work with the ERG to ensure that their actions are aligned with the business goals of the organization.

At the end of the day, I do not want to see ERGs leave. ERGs exist because minority employees are a minority, and they need support to stay and succeed. ERGs are still necessary to build that community for minority employees, but, in my opinion, they're not quite enough. We need one more piece.

Marginalized Employees Need Sponsors

When I left my law firm in 2012 to work for the Illinois Supreme Court, I saved my last goodbye for a partner who had given me one of my first projects early on in my tenure. That one project escalated into another project, then another, then another. The partner introduced me to his clients and to other partners at the firm. He invited me to his lake house and took me out to conferences. He gave me honest feedback when I was struggling, and when I incorporated that feedback into my work, he reviewed it again and took the time to explain to me how I improved. He was the biggest champion that I could ever have had.

When I told him I was leaving the law firm, I cried. I had another calling, but I will always, always, think of that law firm – one of my current clients – with enormous affection. And that has everything to do with a man who was more than my mentor. He was my sponsor.

Most large organizations I work with have some kind of executive coaching for their high-performance minority leaders, but sponsors are different. "Having a sponsor increases the likelihood of being satisfied with the rate of career advancement," notes an article in *Harvard Business Review.* "Conversely, lack of sponsorship increases someone's likelihood of quitting within a year."[11]

Members of marginalized communities *need* sponsors – leaders willing to advocate for us, promote us, defend us, and ensure that biases are interrupted from the first.

Sponsorship is centered on advancing marginalized groups in the workplace to positions of power. The sponsor, therefore, has to be someone with "significant influence" in the organization, and who will advocate for, protect, and fight for the career advancement of the employee that they sponsor.[12]

Or consider this quote from a woman of color:

> I would say I've received a fraction of the opportunities I would have as a White man. The ones that I did receive, I had to fight really hard for. I've seen many White men groomed for leadership. They were hand-held through the process by senior leaders. That didn't mean that they didn't have to perform, but it did mean that the door was open wide for them and they were given all the resources they needed to be successful. That didn't happen for me. I had to literally kick the doors open.[13]

Mentors, Role Models, and Sponsors: What's the Difference?

So how does a sponsor work? Let's use me as an example. Say I'm a mid-level employee at a large corporation, and I'm ready to move up to the next level. To get there, I pick three leaders who can help me: Pari, Brad, and you.

Pari, the Role Model

Pari is a high-level leader I look up to. I'm impressed by her and what she does. Although I've stopped by Pari's office to talk, she's never there, because she's busy and travels constantly. I don't particularly want to have Pari's role in the organization, but I've picked her as a role model because there are so few women at her level here, especially minority women. But Pari doesn't have the time to invest in me even if she wants to, not only because she's so busy but because all the other women of color want her to mentor them, too. So not only is she exhausted from the emotional labor, but she also has to keep hustling herself. That's why Pari should stay my role model. Even if they aren't personally invested in others' success, role models are crucial in the workplace. The old adage that "you can't be what you can't see" is very often true.

Brad, the Mentor

Brad's a few years ahead of me, working up the ladder himself. He's a nice guy, and we work really well together. He's been in my shoes before, so he gives me advice on what to do, where to go, what senior leaders to work with. He introduces me to the right people who give me interesting assignments. I talk to Brad about the challenges I'm facing, and when he has time, he's able to help me and give me advice.

But he's only doing this because he wants to pay it forward. Someone did these things for him, so he wants to do them for someone else. While Brad likes me, he's not really invested in my success. If I leave, it'll be disappointing, but it won't reflect poorly on him or affect his work in any real way. That's why Brad is a mentor. As a mentor, Brad is solely focused on my professional development. His goal is to get me to the point where I can have a sponsor.

That's where you step in.

You, the Sponsor

Finally, there's you. See, you've listened to the talk on bias. You remember Jasmine. You understand the challenges of building an inclusive workforce. And you are a leader willing to do that hard work and make the changes that you know need to happen.

That's why you are a sponsor. Here's what you have.

First, you have clout. You have the social capital to expend on me. You have a powerful voice at the table to speak about and for me. You use that voice to champion me and convince others that I deserve to get those stretch assignments, to meet those high-profile clients, and to be in the space my high-performance has shown I should be in. Your voice supports mine, so when I slip or stumble, I am judged on what I have accomplished, rather than on the mistake that I made.

Second, you believe in me. You believe in what I can achieve. Because you believe in me, you are willing to put your own reputation on the line to support me. I might be a star performer, but I am still as vulnerable to impostor syndrome and stereotype threat and microaggressions as Jasmine. As my sponsor, you know I can reach higher. When promotion opportunities arise, you champion my success. When I want to opt out, you support me opting in. I need to be resilient and confident that I will be able to accomplish this. Having someone like you believing that I can do it, and supporting me in doing it, goes a long way to making that a reality.

Third, you invest in me. Not because you're a philanthropist, but because you expect return. Sponsorship is transactional. You know what my goals are, so you want to know what I can give you for your own professional goals. What new skills am I bringing to the table that you don't have? Maybe I have insight into new technology that you don't understand. Maybe I know about a certain client base that you do not. Maybe I have a skill that you never acquired. Maybe you are seeking to increase your reputational capital in the organization or expand your internal network of support. Whatever it is, both you and I have to identify it and work toward delivering it. Investment requires return. Sponsorship requires that too.

Fourth, you understand my goals and you know what I need to achieve them. You and I together can set out clear expectations of our working relationship. If your goal is to get me to Level X, then we need to define what Level X is, explain what kind of work is needed to get there, then discuss what the success factors are. If I get promoted, what happens after that? If I don't get promoted, what happens after that? Similarly, we need to be clear on what I need to do to make this relationship a success. What should my work product look like? What kind of hours should I be putting in? What contacts do I need to follow up with? Sponsorship isn't low-level support. Sponsorship is high-level strategy.

Finally, you are willing to get uncomfortable. Because cross-gender and cross-cultural relationships are hard and they will require you to get out of your comfort zone and dive into them. Until you are ready to get uncomfortable, that in-group, the team of people who keep working with each other because they like working with each other, they will keep getting ahead.

This is why we need to mention #MeToo. We aren't going to avoid the hard talks. There are many men in the workplace who don't sponsor women or mentor women because of the fact that they are women. Here's what I say to you. If you are sponsoring a woman, you might get that look. There will be people who will assume that your relationship crosses workplace lines into attraction or affairs. That is the reality of gender dynamics in the workplace, particularly when it involves a more senior man and a more junior woman.

That's why sponsorship has to be part of your organization's culture. So people know what to expect. They know the organization has sanctioned these relationships. Then you as the leader set the table. You make it clear why you are investing in me. Make it transparent. Meet in public, keep your door open, and advocate for my skills, so everyone knows that I am a star performer. Most of all, keep being an upstander. When you get that look or hear those comments, stand up and speak about them. Call them out on it. Yes, it will feel uncomfortable, but that's how we change the world.

Because this is the end game, where we move minority employees, fully qualified minority employees, into the positions that they deserve and from which they have been excluded. See, the mountain of inequity is not going to be taken down all at once. It's going to need a strategy, a plan of attack, and piece by piece, we all bring it down together. And while it might take many, many lifetimes to dismantle inequity in the workplace, it only takes one person to start.

You.

Which means there's one last rule of equity for you to learn.

Notes

1. www.forbes.com/sites/janicegassam/2018/10/22/how-to-start-an-employee-resource-group-at-your-organization/#6bea2ca71756
2. https://fairygodboss.com/career-topics/employee-resource-groups

3. https://fairygodboss.com/career-topics/employee-resource-groups
4. https://diversitymbamagazine.com/organizations/companies/nielson/nielsen-holds-leadership-summit-employee-resource-groups/
5. https://fairygodboss.com/career-topics/employee-resource-groups
6. https://fairygodboss.com/career-topics/employee-resource-groups
7. www.cnn.com/2018/11/01/success/employee-resource-groups/index.html
8. www.shrm.org/hr-today/news/hr-magazine/0916/pages/are-employee-resource-groups-good-for-business.aspx
9. www.forbes.com/sites/janicegassam/2018/10/22/how-to-start-an-employee-resource-group-at-your-organization/#6bea2ca71756
10. https://fairygodboss.com/career-topics/employee-resource-groups
11. https://hbr.org/2017/02/diversity-doesnt-stick-without-inclusion
12. www.catalyst.org/wp-content/uploads/2019/01/sponsoring_women_to_success.pdf
13. https://www.mckinsey.com/featured-insights/gender-equality/women-in-the-workplace-2018

Chapter 13

New Rule of Equity #5. Make Authentic Diversity Matter for Good

---

It's a warm summer day in 2013. I'm outside the courthouse in Downtown Chicago. It's Flag Day. I'm standing with about a hundred people around me. Around us, hundreds more are cheering and crying. The hundred people standing with me are all holding their hands over their hearts. We are about to recite an oath. We are about to become American citizens. It was then, and it still is today, one of the happiest days of my entire life.

At the end of 2012, I was finally able to apply for citizenship in a country that I had visited or lived in for the past 20 years, as a tourist, then a student, then a student worker, then a sponsored worker, and then a green cardholder. I could finally be a citizen. I could be an inheritor to the rich, painful, tragic, hopeful, and unending American story. I could vote. I could have a U.S. passport. I could never be deported. I could get federal loans and college assistance. I could work for the federal government. I could travel outside the country for as long as I wanted, and the U.S. embassy would have my back. I could serve on a jury. I could run for any elected office, save one. I could be a judge. In every way, under every law, after being here but apart for so long, I belonged here.

So when the judge in front of us announced, "Congratulations, you are now citizens of the United States of America," I, along with many of us on the Daley Plaza that day, wept. Because we knew, whatever our journeys to get to that day – refugees, immigrants, documented and undocumented, by boat, by plane, by truck, by bus, by foot – that long, long, long journey was over. We hugged. We cried. We shouted. We danced. A few of us collapsed. We were citizens of the United States. We belonged here. No one could take that away from us.

Whenever I ask a judge what the best part of their job is, they always mention that one.

Why We All Need to Belong

Belonging. Even saying that word makes it sound like a fresh breeze carrying a hint of sea air. Say the words "I belong here." Now say them again. That feeling you have when you say that? Of rightness? Of satisfaction? That's how much belonging matters. As humans, our need to belong is hardwired into our DNA.[1] Think back to your childhood: that time you were picked last for a playground team, when no one sat next to you in the lunchroom, or when you found out you weren't invited to a classmate's birthday party. Think about how it felt, *physically* felt, to be left out. Those feelings don't go away when you grow up.

Belonging is the "feeling of value and respect derived from a reciprocal relationship to an external referent that is built on a foundation of shared experiences, beliefs, or personal characteristics."[2] That external referent is *you*. It's your organization, your company, your culture. Belonging means that you share your values and your culture with me, and I in turn share my values and my culture with you. My ability to do that and your ability to create a culture that allows me to do that – both go a long way toward reducing the amount of social exclusion, stigma, and discrimination that I face.

Authentic Lives + Authentic Work = Authentic Diversity

But belonging isn't enough. See, Kevin from Yale belongs. But the other Kevin? Kevin who has anxiety. Kevin of the single mother. Kevin who is undergoing gender transition. Kevin who is deaf. Kevin who doesn't play basketball even though he's Black. Kevin who has an 18-year-old son. Kevin who had to unenroll from college because he couldn't keep his second job. Kevin who suffers from PTSD. Kevin, the authentic Kevin, he wants to belong too. That is where authentic diversity comes in. Authentic diversity is my final rule of equity. Authentic diversity is the last link between equity and inclusion.

Authentic diversity is the ability to bring your authentic self to work, your differences, your identity, and your truth and to not have to leave that at the building door. That's what Kevin wants. That's what Jasmine wants. That's what you should want too. Because diversity without authenticity is diversity without teeth. All those famed benefits of diversity, the different perspectives, the harder thinking, the better problem-solving, all of that only happens if we create an environment where it can take place.

But if the rules of our organization – the dress codes, the languages, the forms of expression, the norms, the values, the emotional processes, the intellectual processes – keep telling us that no, diversity matters, but only in name alone, then how quickly do we realize that we need to cover, to assimilate, and to mask, that we can't stop doing it, until we live that duality our whole lives, we stall in place, or until we leave. That's what authenticity is. Authenticity is the difference between saying diversity matters and making it matter.

Now I know authenticity gets a bad rap. "Authenticity means you can show up wearing ripped jeans and flip flops," someone grumbles. Let's correct that right now.

First, authenticity isn't about what you look like. Wearing ripped jeans and flip flops can be just as performative as wearing a suit and tie every day. Authenticity is instead about who *you* are. What *your* values are. What actions *you* have taken in your life. What choices *you* have made. How all of those have combined to create the person *you* are today.

Second, authenticity isn't about you as an individual any more than belonging is about you as an individual. Authenticity is always relational; it's about you as a part of a community. It's in your interactions with others. It's understanding how your present and past actions have influenced other people and whether those actions and the values you have because of them, match up with how you interact with your community.

Authenticity means that you are not consistently regulating your behavior and your emotional expressions.[3] That's the mental labor that Kevin has to do every day just so he can belong. That labor, instead, gets re-directed into his work, which means Kevin serves his customers better, his clients better, and his leadership better. He doesn't have to constantly refresh his tank. He knows that he is living in accordance with his values in how he relates to others. He has a genuine sense of "psychological safety," the confidence that his team will not embarrass, reject, or punish him for speaking up," where they trust and respect each other and are comfortable being themselves and sharing their opinions.[4]

Authenticity matters. It matters for diversity. It matters for inclusion. It matters if you are going to transform outcomes for the real people who you are leading. Authentic diversity. It's how we change the workplace for good.

Authentic Diversity Means Sharing Your Truths at Work

Authenticity starts with you. As a leader, a leader who centers their diversity on people, I want you to think about the power you have to make authenticity matter for everyone. Open up about your life, your struggles, your successes, and your truths. That's what Tim Cook did at Apple. In 2014, he publicly came out as a gay man in a magazine article. Here's what he had to say:

> [If] hearing that the CEO of Apple is gay can help someone struggling to come to terms with who he or she is, or bring comfort to anyone who feels alone, or inspire people to insist on their equality, then it's worth the trade-off with my own privacy.[5]

We can't keep telling people to keep their authentic lives out of the workplace. It's too late to not talk about difference. It's too late to pretend that we aren't different. And us continuing to do that, continuing to sit in the workplace and pretend we're all the same just means that the people who are different, who don't fit into the accepted mainstream, will be left out.

Plus, it's only going to get harder. As the pandemic has demonstrated, the geographical lines between work and home are fully blurred. Many of us work from home. Many of us use social media to check on our lives. We have pictures of our kids and families and pets. We go home, and we check emails and check into work. This is the reason so many office buildings are trying to replicate the home, with food and drinks and games, because they recognize that the space between work and home is vanishing. Work is everywhere around us, in us, it's everywhere we go, on vacation, at home, at our kids' basketball games. We can't keep on trying to push our personal selves out.

We all have stories to share. It's time to share them. If you as a leader start out by sharing your authentic stories, you will help create that "psychological safety" in the workplace. Once you set the table, the people who work with you can feel comfortable enough, and safe enough, to do so as well.

Dave grew up playing travel hockey every weekend in the suburbs. Pari grew up going to Indian weddings every weekend in the suburbs. Kevin grew up with four siblings and a single mom in a one-bedroom apartment in the city. Jake got married to his college sweetheart too, but had to wait until his country legalized same-sex marriage. Jasmine has two kids, and it's really hard when she has to log back in to work at 10 pm and pretend it's OK. Kim has multiple sclerosis and hides her motorized scooter when she arrives at work. Ibrahim prays five times a day, and he does it in the windowless conference room so no one sees him.

Authenticity means the challenges of having a child aren't something I have to hide. Where I am a man who can bring his husband to the holiday party and not feel uncomfortable doing so. Where I can wear my natural Black curly hair and not have everyone ask, for the millionth time, "Did you cut it?" Where the fact that I recruit at my church brunch is just as appreciated as when I recruit at the golf course. Where I don't have to apologize to my company that I can't make the company-wide meeting, because it's scheduled for sunset on Eid. Where even though my disability is not visible, it doesn't mean that I don't struggle with it every single day. Where being the first in my family to go to college isn't something I have to hide; it's something that helps me belong.

That's what I mean when I say authentic lives. But authentic lives are only half the authentic diversity equation.

Authentic Diversity Means Marginalized Employees Incorporate Their Values into Their Work

We need to take those authentic lives and make space for authentic work. How do we do that? Start with this: understand your organizational culture.

Examine the Culture That Surrounds You

Go back to Old Rule of Diversity #5. Think about your workplace culture. See, culture is often an invisible concept. I like the analogy of water to a fish. A lot of us don't know just how deeply ingrained our cultures are in us. Just like water to a fish, our culture's influence is often invisible to us.[6] It is simply what we know and what we depend on for survival. It's when we come out of the water that we realize how much we relied on it. It's because it's so invisible that it makes it so difficult for us to see it. It also makes it easy for us to fall back on Old Rule #5 – that everyone is welcome in our culture.

Here's one way to think about it. What's the first thing you do when you enter an elevator? You turn around, and you stare at the doors. That is a cultural norm. But what if you were standing in an elevator and someone entered and stood right in front of you, face to face with you. You would feel uncomfortable. You would gasp. You would think they were strange. Because they are violating cultural norms. They are not abiding by the social contract that we have with each other. That's how culture works. For doing nothing more than standing the exact way people stand on crowded subway trains.

What's the elevator rule in your organization? What are the norms that govern your social contract? Answer these questions for me. When it comes to your organization, what behaviors are expressed? What relationships are allowed? How do you greet each other? What is considered polite and impolite? How closely do you stand with each other? How do you show respect and disrespect? Is privacy desirable or undesirable? Who makes what decisions and in what circumstances? What should be communicated directly or indirectly, and to whom?[7]

I could ask dozens more like these, but I hope they give you a good enough starting point. Those questions are intended to elucidate what precisely your culture is. Read through them. Make a list of your answers. Then think about if you sat down with your colleagues and you all answered those questions, how similar your lists would be. You know what your workplace culture is like. You know what your workplace culture expects. You know what norms exist here.

Because your organization has a culture. A culture of policies, procedures, programs, and processes. Those cultures are going to incorporate certain values, beliefs, assumptions, and customs. How are meetings run? How do we obtain work? How do we share credit? How do we promote ourselves? How do we mentor each other? Doors open or doors closed? Talking over each other or waiting for the other person to speak first? What holidays do we celebrate? What neighborhoods do we live in, particularly the people in management? What pictures can we bring into our offices? What interactions are we allowed to have, and with whom? How top-down is our workplace? Is competition rewarded over collaboration? Is individualism rewarded over teamwork? Is self-advocacy rewarded over humility? Is isolation rewarded over community? Is institutional knowledge rewarded over formal processes?

All of these are different aspects of work culture. And like I said in Old Rule #5, the culture of many organizations is quite simply the culture of the majority. In the case of most of corporate America, it is the culture of the White majority men who built these workplaces, whether they were traditionalists in Scranton, or millennials in Silicon Valley. Like the people facing the back of an elevator, who have immediately violated a social contract, the majority culture doesn't often lend itself to incorporating others.

Recognize the Values That Have Built Your Culture

Now we're going to step away from your organization for a bit. We're going to focus on you. I would like you to think through the values around which you center your life. There are hundreds of values you can think of. Pick five and make a list. Fortitude. Hard Work. Self-reliance. Achievement. Boldness. Sincerity. Legacy. Challenge. Comfort. Control. Family. Growth. Joy. Trust. Charity. Tradition. Risk. Financial Stability. Success.

Think about which values matter the most to you. Think about how you're allowed to express them at your organization. Think about why you have them. Where they came from. What your parents instilled in you.

Now go back to your organization culture. Remember that first list you made, of what cultural norms are accepted in your organization? The list that's similar to your colleague's? Well, your colleague made a second list, just like you did, of values that matter to them. Think about how similar your first list of cultural norms is to your colleague's. Then think about how different your second list of values might be. Because while you and your colleague work in a similar culture in your organization, you may have had very different values that have shaped who you both are.

Here's why that matters. For many people, especially those from marginalized communities, the values that they bring in the door may not match the culture that is exhibited in the workplace. Because authenticity is not just in the clothes you wear, the shoes you have on, or your style of hair. It is also in the values you have. Your values which do not change, whether you are at home or at work. And if you are Kevin or Jasmine or Ibrahim, then the real question becomes this: are your values welcomed in your workplace culture?

Because I know, I hope, that if you are in the majority in your workplace, then you have values that reflect in the work that you do. And it is entirely possible that the value is revenue generation. It's success. It's a comfortable retirement. It's being politically active. It's sending your children through college. It's serving on non-profit boards. It's leaving a legacy behind. If you are a White man, part of your privilege of being a White man in the American workplace is working in an organization culture where those values are reflected – in the way work is done, processes are structured, and success is recognized – because that organization was built by and for people like you.

This is why I am asking you this. Please take a step back. Look at the culture you have in your workplace. Look hard at it and recognize that the work culture that you think fits everyone was never really meant to include everyone.

Welcome to Inclusion

"How long?"

See, Jasmine's question isn't just about when she can use her real dialect and listen to her type of music and wear her hair with its natural curl. It's also about how she talks to clients. How she collaborates in teams. How she receives and delivers feedback. How she manages her work. How she incorporates her children into her work life. How she talks to supervisors. How she prioritizes projects. How she reaches out to leads. How the values that she has – faith, family, community, stewardship, empathy, justice – impact the work that she does. That's the authentic diversity she wants to find in your workplace.

If you as a leader want to help her do that, then once you have figured out what your culture is, figure out what it is your clients and customers need from you. Whether this culture you've identified, how essential it is to your organization's success. Why did your clients hire you? What value do you deliver to them? What do you better than your competitors? Why do they keep coming back to you? And crucially, how much of this culture is your clients, and how much is it just doing it the way it's always been done, the way that's comfortable for the people who run it, and not for the people who stay quiet or leave?

You want diversity to really matter? To go beyond the pronouncements and the scholarships and the dinners and the awards? Then create a workplace that recognizes, celebrates, and accepts difference, that is comfortable with different values, and that allows people to incorporate those different values into the work they do.

Because we are all different. We have different lives. We come from different spaces. We communicate differently. We compete differently. We work differently. That's what diversity is. But we're trying to put on these masks that just don't fit many of us and were never intended to.

Which is my final challenge for you in this book. You as a leader need to create a workplace where diversity matters. Where the people who work at your organization are trusted enough to be creative and use their own judgments on how to complete their work, while still fitting in with what your customers need and your goals as an organization. It is a difficult goal to achieve. I never said this was going to be an easy journey. But that is exactly what authentic work is. Work that's owned by your employees. Work that incorporates their values. Work that they are excited about. Work that they are engaged with. Work they can be creative with. Work that all still exists with what your clients and your organization need to succeed.

But Michelle, you tell me. Everyone has to adapt to a workplace culture. I agree, they do. I remember in college when I was getting ready for my internship at the United Nations in Geneva. I had never had an office job in my entire life, other than my college work-study jobs. So 19-year-old Michelle had to figure out what was appropriate office wear for the United

Nations. Where did I go? Up to this point, all my clothes were purchased exclusively from Wal-Mart, so I decided to shop where I had seen all my other friends shop – Forever 21. A few days after my shopping trip I walked into the apartment of an older friend of mine and I showed her the fringe top and cutoff jeans that I had bought for the UN and she burst out laughing. "Michelle! You can't wear this to the UN!" She was right. Because there was a culture that I was expected to understand. That is the price of living in any civilization.

Adaptation is fine. But recognize that you are asking people to make a choice and for some people, that choice to adapt might be much harder than it would be for those whose values match your workplace. And recognize that for others, you aren't asking them to adapt. You are instead Henry Ford telling Kevin from Yale to assimilate to succeed. You're asking him to jump into that melting pot, to transform, and to come out as a White majority male version of himself.

If you want to keep hiring and promoting people who share the same values as you, and who will easily feel comfortable in a workplace that was built for them, then by all means, keep at it. But if you want to recruit, retain, and lead a workplace centered on equity, then find a way to allow people who are different have their values matter in your workplace as well. That is authentic diversity. Create a workplace centered on that. Here's what you get in return.

You get innovation, where people want to explore new ideas and new possibilities and are encouraged to do so. You get investment, where people are invested in your organization and the culture you develop together, where people own the work they do, and where they feel responsible for what they created. You get production, where people know what your organization needs to do to be successful, and they continually improve to make that better. You get success, where people have more and more autonomy, use that to design work they are engaged in, work they take risks with, and work that is authentic to them.[8]

Most of all, you get people who stay. You get to look at your competitors and see that they are failing the #ten-yearchallenge over and over again, while you have employees in your organization who brought their authentic selves to work, who owned the authentic work they did, and who had the resources they needed to succeed. That's inclusion. That's authenticity. And that's how we change the workplace for good.

Notes

1. www.ncbi.nlm.nih.gov/pubmed/15740417
2. Mahar, A. L., Cobigo, V., & Stuart, H. (2013). Conceptualizing belonging. *Disability and Rehabilitation, 35*(12), 1026–1032.
3. Grandey, A., Foo, S. C., Groth, M., & Goodwin, R. E. (2012). Free to be you and me: a climate of authenticity alleviates burnout from emotional labor. *Journal of Occupational Health Psychology, 17*(1), 1.
4. Edmondson, Amy (June 1999). Psychological safety and learning behavior in work teams. *Administrative Science Quarterly, 44*(2), 350–383, 354.
5. www.bloomberg.com/news/articles/2014-10-30/tim-cook-speaks-up
6. Building Cultural Competence: Innovative Activities and Models, Kate Berardo, Darla K. Deardorff, Stylus Publishing, LLC., Jun 1, 2012
7. http://jonfreach.com/essays/2018/3/24/66-way-we-differ
8. If you want a more in-depth explanation of these concepts and how authenticity leads directly to employee productivity and success, please read Robin Ryde and Lisa Sofiano, *Creating Authentic Organizations*. (Kogan Page, 2014)

Chapter 14

Goodbye from the 70th Floor

I'm back in your office. It's getting near lunchtime now. You haven't said anything for the past hour, while you've listened to me talk about these new rules of equity, and the only solution I can possibly see to the inclusion crisis in corporate America. Your head is down. I stop talking. A minute passes. Then you lift up your head, and like Jasmine all those years ago, you say two simple words: "Thank you."

I nod and I stand up. I need to give you some time. You have a lot to think about. Much of it is seeing the world in a different way than the way you imagined it because I am not giving you the story that Jasmine has heard all her life. That *she* needs to change. That *she* needs to lean in. That *she* needs to pull herself up by her bootstraps.

No, this is a different story. This is the story not from the perspective of those who have succeeded; it's from those who have not. It's the story where you don't gaslight them. Where you don't say, "This can't be true." Where you realize that you have benefited enormously from the systems in place in your organization and those who haven't succeeded; well, it can't be the systems that are the problem. Because that would mean the systems aren't fair. They aren't equal. That we aren't on an even playing field. That there are equally talented, intelligent, hard-working people who are not succeeding not because of anything that's wrong with them but because bias, racism, privilege, and a culture so close to my own, have all allowed me to succeed. Understanding what all that really means is an extraordinarily hard reckoning to have.

I stand up, I shake your hand and I leave, because here's what I hope will happen next. In two days, in a week, in a month, you're going to call me. You're going to be excited. You're going to be nervous. You're going to be hopeful. You're going to tell me, "Michelle. I'm going to do this. I am going to change the workplace for good." I smile because now, you *are* all the way on board. But I'm going to ask you one more question before you start. "What is your why?"

What Is Your Why?

If you are committing to this path to inclusion, ripping out systems of inequity from their very foundations, then I need you to tell me why. Because my voice, as strong and loud as it may be, will never be as strong as yours. Which of the old rules resonated with you? Which of the new ones did? For the space that you are in? For the work that you do? For the shareholders you have to convince? For the leadership you need to bring along? For the employees you do not wish to alienate? For the work that you are committing to?

For you reading this, that's my question to you. What is your why? What is the reason you have for building an workplace centered on equity? Because I do not know you. I do not know your organization. I do not know your employees. I do not know your shareholders. I do not know your friends, your kids, or your spouse. I do not know if you're the senator of a state or a union organizer in the Southwest.

But I know you picked up this book for a reason. I know that you chose it because you want to see change. I know that when we started, you weren't sure what to do or how to get there. And I also know for sure that the only person who can convince you of what to do is you. That's why I need you to know your why.

Remember those values I spoke about earlier? Find your why there. Remember your commitment to antiracism? Find your why there. Remember the culture of your workplace? Find your why there. Remember those kids you are raising? Find your why there. Remember that business case that you made? Find your why there. Remember that data that you gathered? Find your why there. Remember the people you are leading? Find your why there. When we started, I said we were taking a journey. This is your map, but the journey is yours to take. And no one, no one, starts any kind of journey unless they have a reason to take it.

Why are you doing this? Because people are going to doubt you. They won't want you to hire that older female UX designer who doesn't have as much experience as the five young men hired last month. They'll get upset when they find out that the Asian-American man was assigned a sponsor and they were not. They'll get frustrated at learning new evaluation systems. They'll feel uncomfortable when you say the joke they made was offensive, it was hurtful, and it was wrong. That's why I want to know *your* why. Because you will feel like stopping this work, that you truly have everything to lose by doing this, nothing to lose by going back to the way it was before, and that while you empathize with Jasmine, it's just too hard to keep changing the workplace for her.

What is your why? I'm going to tell you mine, and then I'm going to let you go.

Chapter 15

Change the Workplace for Good

When I tell people the story of why I do this work, I usually start with Jasmine. But my journey started earlier than that. It starts in 2001, with an airplane flight that changed my life. I'll tell you the story now, for two reasons. One, because this story is my "why." It is my hope for the workplace and our world. Two, because perhaps one of you reading this book will know someone who was on this flight. If you do, please tell them thank you from me.

Picture it. Concourse D. Miami Airport. January 2001. Now, if you've ever been to Concourse D in the Miami Airport, it is, despite the enormous work put in by Miami-Dade County, just a nightmare to make a connection in, especially if you are connecting from an international flight. And in 2001, it was even worse.

At this point in 2001, my mother had left Jamaica and moved to Botswana. The year 2001 was also before I had a credit card or a cell phone. Honestly, it was before most people my age had cell phones.

Here we are. January 2001. A few days after New Year's Day. I'm flying from Jamaica to Miami to New York to get back to school at Princeton. This is the first time I've done this trip by myself. Once I get off the plane in New York, I have to get on the shuttle bus (money) to the subway (money) to Penn Station where I would then take the New Jersey Transit train (money) to Princeton, and then change to the Princeton Dinky Shuttle (money) to get to school. If you can't tell from my parentheticals, this entire journey would require money. Which was fine! Because I have just enough money to get back to school. Everything was fine.

Until it wasn't. After racing, and I mean racing, to get out of immigration to make my connection from Miami to JFK, I reach the gate just in time. I reach into my backpack to get my passport and boarding pass. As the crush of people rush pass me to get to their own distant gates, I feel a brush on my side. I look down. My wallet has been stolen out of my pocket.

Money. Money. Money. Money. Money. And now I have none. I have no way of making that shuttle to the subway to the train to the other train to school. No way. And again, no cell phone. And again, mother in Botswana. And, of course, no phone number for my mother in Botswana because that's at school. And none of this matters because this flight is boarding right now and I can't do anything except get on that plane. So what do I do instead?

I break down and cry. I'm 18 years old, and this is the worst thing that could ever happen to me. I would never get back to school, I would miss my exams, Princeton would kick me out, no one would find me, I'd be wandering around New York, my mother would be terrified, everything was a spiraling disaster, and I have no idea what to do.

There's only one thing I can do. My flight to New York is leaving. I have to get on. I go up, the last person to board, and get on my plane. At least I still have my passport and boarding pass. I walk down the jet bridge, still sobbing. As I get on the plane, the flight attendant sees me. Before I can board, she steps outside on the jet bridge and asks me a simple question, "Honey, what's wrong?"

"WAAAHHHHHHHH!" is my first response.

"Ohhh, ok," she says. "Take a breath. Tell me what's wrong."

I tell her. I tell her that my wallet was stolen, my mom being scared, not being able to get back to school, how I will be lost in New York, the dogs will eat my body; and I'm amazed that she can even understand a word that I'm saying because I am crying so hard. But she does. She gives me a hug. Then she looks at me and says, "Don't worry about it. We got you."

She walks me to an empty seat in the back of the plane. She sits me down. She gets me a glass of water and then goes to the front to tell the pilot we're ready to go.

The flight takes off. But in my head, I'm still running through all the horrific "what if" possibilities. No money. No money. No money. No money.

The flight levels off. The pilot's voice comes over the intercom. He says what he typically says for a flight, "This is going to be a great flight to New York," and so on. Then he says something else, something that I have never forgotten.

"Well, this is going to be a great flight, except for one person. You see, her wallet was stolen, and she's just trying to get back to school. I know if you were her mom, you'd want to know she got back to school safe. So I'm going to pass around my pilot's hat. If you could put any money you can in it for her, I want to tell her mom that we got her back safely."

He did exactly that. And the people on that flight raised $300 for me. I did get back to school, safe and sound.

That is my why. That is why I do the work I do. That's my truth. And it defines my current work and the spaces in which I lead because I believe in us. I believe in you. You reading this book there. I have to. I believe you can do more than change the workplace. I believe you can change the world.

It is a lot easier to give a few dollars to a scared child trying to get home, than to end inequity in the world. We haven't even addressed the disparities in health access, wages, housing, and education that we will need to end as well. This is not easy work. Every time you step forward, you will feel like you stumble five steps back. You want to give the people who are following you nice packages with easy resolutions and happy endings, but that's not the reality of the workplace or the world.

Remember my Flag Day story from the previous chapter? I tell that story. And I tell another one. It was almost exactly one month later that a jury of my new fellow American citizens found the man who had killed Trayvon Martin not guilty of his murder. One month later when they decided that Trayvon's Black life, my Black life, and the Black lives of millions of Americans, did not matter.

It is easier to donate money to a scared kid than to dismantle unequal and unfair systems. And yet. At the very core of this work of equity is what that pilot asked on that plane. To empathize with another person. To care about another person's life. To recognize that you have the power to change someone's life. And to understand that someone's else success and ability to thrive is as equal to yours. That they matter too.

That's my why. I believe in a world where we support each other, where we carry each other when we stumble, and where we ensure that no one, absolutely no one, gets left behind.

That's my why. What is yours?

Because our world is changing. Our workplaces are changing. You have a choice. You can either stay behind, or you can march ahead. Like the great leaders of change who have come before you, I hope you march.

As you march, remember the old rules of diversity. The ones that cannot stand. We should only make the very bare minimum of the business case; say bias is fine and that's OK; never, ever talk about race; assume everyone starts at the same starting line, and that our culture includes everyone. Knock those old rules down on your march.

Replace them with the new rules of equity. Center inclusion on people, implement a data-driven equity strategy, use competencies to find the "right fit," build a community with employee resource groups that work and sponsors that advocate for success, and, most of all, make space for authentic lives and authentic work. That's how we change the workplace for good.

Take those new rules and march. March into your offices, into your companies, into your schools, into your boards. Use these new rules to create spaces where everyone can confidently enter and be told this truth: "You belong here and I am willing to do the hard work to make sure you stay and succeed."

Because it's been two years since I last saw Jasmine and when she sees me again and asks, "Michelle, how long?" I want to tell her, "Not much longer," because people like you are working to change the world.

I always called it equity, changing the rules to ensure fairness and equality. But then I heard a word recently that I liked a lot more.

Justice.

As leaders, keep justice at the core of every authentic space you lead, and make it the starring role of the legacy that you leave behind. I can't wait to see the world that awaits when you do.

Index

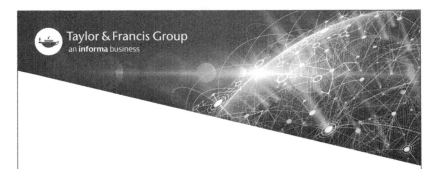

Made in the USA
Middletown, DE
11 September 2020